# PUTIN'S PRISONER

www.penguin.co.uk

# PUTIN'S PRISONER

*My Time as a Prisoner of War in Ukraine*

Aiden Aslin with John Sweeney

bantam

TRANSWORLD PUBLISHERS
Penguin Random House, One Embassy Gardens,
8 Viaduct Gardens, London SW11 7BW
www.penguin.co.uk

Transworld is part of the Penguin Random House group of companies
whose addresses can be found at global.penguinrandomhouse.com

Penguin
Random House
UK

First published in Great Britain in 2023 by Bantam
an imprint of Transworld Publishers

A CIP catalogue record for this book
is available from the British Library.

ISBNs
9780857505293 hb
9780857505309 tpb

Typeset in 14/17 pt Bembo Book MT Pro by Jouve (UK), Milton Keynes
Printed and bound in Great Britain by Clays Ltd, Elcograf S.p.A.

The authorized representative in the EEA is Penguin Random House Ireland,
Morrison Chambers, 32 Nassau Street, Dublin D02 YH68.

Penguin Random House is committed to a sustainable future for our business, our readers and our
planet. This book is made from Forest Stewardship Council® certified paper.

To Diana, to my fallen comrades
and those still in captivity and to a free Ukraine

*And that's the place where we, benign*
*In our great mercy, hunted down*
*Pathetic freedom — naked, gaunt —*
*And set the dogs on it. The bones*
*Of many soldiers languish there.*
*And what of blood, and what of tears?*

'The Caucasus' by Taras Shevchenko
Translated by Alyssa Dinega Gillespie

# CONTENTS

# Foreword

One of the most dramatic videos showing the horror of Russia's war against Ukraine appeared on the internet in the spring of 2022. An unknown Briton filmed himself in the ruins of the Illich steelworks in Mariupol, saying that his Ukrainian army commanders had given the order to surrender after weeks of being surrounded, their food and ammo gone. The Briton was Aiden Aslin and he behaved very bravely, but his eyes looked into a dark and uncertain future.

A few days later, in another video, Aiden appeared with a smashed-up face testifying to unknown people. The Russians turned his fate into a perverted reality show. Satisfying the needs of their audience for bloody revenge, they sentenced him to death. The Russian newspapers were cock-a-hoop, savouring Aiden's anxiety, his fears about execution. They made him sing the Russian national anthem and this video of his humiliation was shared far and wide. But what happens in Russia or Russian-occupied Ukraine when the camera is turned off? This is not just a question that arises when you see a video like the one made by Aiden in Russian captivity. It is the only question.

'You do know that if I am taken prisoner, I will tell everything right away? I'm just warning you guys.' That's what a friend told me while we were preparing to go to war. It was a joke but our laughter had a nervous edge to it. Captivity is scary. Before battle, you think about what might happen to you. For us, it is more terrible to be captured than to die a quick death. Especially when you are captured by the Russians.

During this bloody war, a war that has been going on since 2014, I have had to watch several Russian videos of interrogations with people I knew personally. A guy I studied with at school looked into the camera; he was scared, and told how he was forced to sit in an army tank, that the Ukrainian commanders had deceived and threatened him, that Ukrainian commanders were sending people to be slaughtered, that Ukraine was oppressing the Russian language.

I saw how a burnt, injured neighbour of my grandmother proudly and courageously answered the questioning of Russian propagandists.

But, more often, people break. I have heard how cruel they were to the Ukrainian writer Stanislav Aseyev in a Donetsk concentration camp. I know what a 'black dolphin' is – the prisoner's head bent low, his arms handcuffed behind his back, so that movement is agony. I have listened to a speech by a therapist working with young Ukrainian soldiers who, captured by the Russians, have been castrated.

Therefore, before battle, for my friends and I, capture is considered worse than death.

If I have to admit that the Russians have some special talent inherent in their nation, it is the ability to equip prisons and torture chambers. Ukrainians at a subconscious level know this and therefore it is impossible to find a person in our country who is capable of condemning a prisoner for collaborating with the executioners.

Being heroic in a Russian prison can only be imagined by someone who does not have the slightest chance of ending up in one.

Someone who saved himself after such humiliation, torture and daily fear of death is a heroic character for me. It is painful to listen to and read their stories, but it is also necessary because reality always requires a direct and strong look. You have to look a predator in the eye and modern Russia is obviously a bloody and unprincipled predator.

Read Aiden's book.

Vlad Demchenko, Ukrainian Special Forces,
Bakhmut, May 2023

# CHAPTER ONE

# Funtopia

One of our guys doing guard watch, 'Popeye', has his radio with him and the call comes through: '*Vosdukh!*' – 'Air raid!'

I continue smoking my borrowed pipe, looking like Gandalf, waiting for the bomb.

Whoosh! Written down it sounds kind of fun, but the reality is anything but. We hear a muffled bang, lots of metal-on-metal clattering but no proper explosion.

I take the pipe out of my mouth and say: 'No boom?'

One of the guys runs in from the top of the stairs, out of breath, and yells: '*Pizdiets!*' Loosely translated as 'Fuck!'

That doesn't help us understand what has happened much. Or, indeed, at all. After he recovers his breath, he tells us that a bomb has been dropped on our ammunition dump but, luckily, it didn't go off. Then we hear a Russian fighter come in for a second run. Everyone freezes. No sound is made other than the scream of the jet, then 'Whoosh!'

This time it goes: 'Boom! Boom! BOOM!' The bomb

not only explodes, it hits our ammo dump on the nose. While we've still been thinking about a breakout from the siege of Mariupol, two lorries have been loaded with what's left of our ammo: bullets, mortar bombs, mines, Javelins, NLAWs, Stingers, the whole bloody works, tons of the stuff. The Russian bomb hits the ammo lorries and all of our explosives blow up in a series of secondary explosions more terrifying, because of their mass, than the one Russian bomb. In the military, we call this 'cooking' and it's bloody frightening. I first came across explosives cooking in Syria when the Americans bombed our Kurdish unit by mistake. The only thing you can do is hide.

Everything is gone. All we had left was in those two lorries. To make matters worse, when the Russians see our ammunition cooking off high into the sky, their tanks join in the fun, raking the steelworks with shell after shell. The pressure wave from every shell is extraordinarily powerful, worse than when you're standing too close to the edge of the platform when an express train speeds through a station in the countryside. The air burst now releases great storm clouds of dust, which rain down on us. Bits of the steelworks start falling down too.

You couldn't go above ground. It's too dangerous. Everyone is told: 'Stay underground.'

I love the Illich iron- and steelworks here in Mariupol. Compared to our old hole in the ground in the middle of nowhere, it is fascinating, like living inside the set of *Blade Runner*. Or better, the secret base below ground where the humans hide from the machines in *The Matrix*. Pipes run this way and that; immense crane platforms on huge wheels stand poised to move great steel pipes; furnaces are still damping down. The place is huge, a city within a city. The plant was first opened in 1896 by two Americans who had got permission from the tsar to make the steel for railway lines and ships and pipes. It had last seen battle in 1944 when the Red Army had kicked the Nazis out of Mariupol. And now, incredible to think of this happening in the twenty-first century, it is hosting another.

The steelworks is getting such a hammering from the Russian tanks that we start worrying whether the roof will fall in and we could be buried underground. The medics are having a terrible time dealing with the injured. They are fast running out of essential supplies, especially the key drugs to ease soldiers in agony.

The hardest thing to bear is the dread written on everyone's faces. Without ammo, all hope is gone. We are fucked, utterly. I feel sick with fear, we all do. Our battalion commander, Major Yevhenii Bova, walks into our bunker, alone, sits on a chair, and smokes a cigarette while around four hundred of us stare at him in silence.

Nothing is said. Nothing has to be said. We are defeated.

The tanks shell the steelworks for two hours straight. Night falls and by 9 p.m. yet more people from the front line have retreated into our bunker. Word is that we are cut off from the other Ukrainian units in the city. I go to try to sleep, not knowing what will be in store for us during the night ahead.

'Johnny, get up.' (The Ukrainians can't handle 'Aiden'.) I'm woken around midnight by David, my oppo (opposite number) in our mortar unit in the Ukrainian Marines. Our company commander, Lieutenant Volodyslav, comes over and speaks to me in English: 'Johnny, you've got an important decision to make. You've got three choices. One, come with me and we're going to try to break out in the vehicles. Two, walk out on foot with another group. Three, stay here with the injured. And then, tomorrow, surrender. You have ten minutes to decide.'

These are the words I had dreaded. Originally, I was up for a breakout, but when that fell through, I'd got cold feet more than ever. In Syria I had witnessed ISIS fighters in vehicles trying to break out and they had been slaughtered by a combination of air strikes and artillery. Leaving on foot is the better option.

'How many are getting out by foot?' I ask the lieutenant.

'A lot,' he replies.

That's bad news. There's no way a large group of people would be able to get out on foot, unnoticed. Safety past Ukrainian lines – that's 140 kilometres away.

'I'm going to stay and surrender with the others,' I say. My logic is that it would be better for me to officially surrender than be caught by some ragtag Russian unit who would love nothing better than to kill me at first sight. I grab my power-bank chargers and some MREs (Meals Ready to Eat) I have saved and give them to the lieutenant, wishing him good luck. We shake hands.

Some of the guys who are going to break out are packing, ready to slip out into the night. Who is left? There are dozens of injured, ranging from people who have been lightly wounded to double amputees who need proper medical attention urgently. But the large majority, around five hundred of the six hundred in the battalion, are going to surrender. I am a little surprised.

There is no internet, no phone signal, and I have a ton of data on SD or flash memory cards logging Russian war crimes. If the Russians catch me with this, things will not go well for me. I have to destroy all the good work I have done. It is so bleak. I go through all my pockets, collect all my SD cards and start breaking them in two. I unscrew my camera from its lens and smash it to the ground. It doesn't break. I won't lie, I have always been pitifully anxious about the camera getting even a little scratch and now I am throwing it against a concrete floor and the fucking thing keeps on bouncing back, unscathed. Now I put my back into it, clubbing the camera against a concrete wall until the casing shatters. I smash the inner lens and snap the screen off, and then I throw my beloved camera into a mess of steel pipes in a disused corner of the factory.

I sit on the bed and take my phone out and start deleting everything. I then go into my settings and do a factory reset. Everything I have covered and documented in Mariupol: gone.

The hopes I had that I would get it out and show the world what Russia had done to Mariupol: gone.

My ambition to be some kind of war reporter or filmmaker: all gone.

I am getting ready to smash my phone but for some reason hold off doing so. Then I catch a glimpse of the corner of the bunker and see an ordinary soldier, not an officer, standing next to the new command room. They have switched the Starlink back on so the high-ups can talk to the Ukrainian army high command. I ask the lone guy what the password is and he gives it to me.

I am so pissed off at myself. Had I known they would switch the internet back on, I would have sent all my data to friends around the world, then deleted everything. Now I'm connected to the internet with nothing to use, no numbers to call, no email, Instagram or Twitter accounts. All my social media accounts need an SMS code which has been erased. I have been locked out of my own Instagram account by my friend Regent, when I told him I was going dark. I am locked out of everything with no way to contact my loved ones and let them know what is happening. I open Facebook and create a throw-away account and take a quick selfie.

I look worn out, tired, dirty. I know what is coming and what awaits me. I start sending random messages to friends whose details I could remember and keep spamming people until I get an answer. The early hours in Ukraine are the middle of the night in Britain. Everyone is asleep. I have no idea how long the internet will last.

Message after message is sent. Nowt. Then an old pal, Brennan, accepts.

'Bro pick UP i need to speak ASAP!' He picks up and I say: 'Hey bro? I don't have much time. I need you to try to wake my family up. Tell them to add me and call me asap. We are surrendering. Please bro!' He is distressed because we haven't spoken for some time, and out of the blue I call him and lay heavy news on him. He's coming back to

Ukraine after a spell away from the front line and his voice is consoling, telling me that I am going to be OK.

Silence.

'Hello, are you there?' Brennan asks.

'They will use me for their bullshit propaganda,' I reply. And they do.

I get through to Diana, my Ukrainian fiancée. She has just woken up. I can tell by her voice she has already been told what's happening. I won't lie, I don't know what to say. I just tell her: 'I love you so much and I'm going to promise you I will come back to you. I just need you to know, it could take a few months, even a year, but no matter what, I will come home to you.'

As I tell her that, part of me knows that it's a lie and that, most likely, I am going to die.

'I love you,' and then I have to go.

Once I hang up the phone, I take a deep breath and hold back my tears. I go to the hangar and film my proof-of-life surrender video. It captures my mood. It's bleak beyond the saying of it: 'If you are watching this, it means we've surrendered.'

We have run out of ammunition, food and hope. Even the boldest of the Ukrainian troops don't fancy their chances making it 140 kilometres across country, but I'm a Brit. My ability with Russian is coming on, however, the moment I open my mouth people know that I'm not a local.

I turn towards the light in the steelworks and behind me a fire is burning viciously. There's a catch in my voice as I knock out my final video as a free man. I send it to my mum and she sends it to friends, so it's posted from my Twitter and Instagram accounts that I have locked myself out of. My handle is @cossackgundi: 'Cossack' because the Ukrainian Cossacks ruled the country in the eighteenth century, even going so far as to burn down Moscow. And 'gundi' meaning 'farmer' or 'peasant' in Kurdish because, before coming to Ukraine, I fought with the Kurds against Islamic State in Syria: @cossackgundi tells the story of my whole life in two words joined together as one. I'm worried that I might not last another two hours. I have no sense of it at the time but my social media presence, one of the biggest of the British volunteers fighting with Ukraine, has caught the attention of someone high up in the Kremlin.

The words fall from my lips as heavy as lead: 'We didn't have any other choice other than to surrender. Hopefully this fucking war finishes so that fucking peace can come again. Hopefully the Ukrainian Marines will be treated accordingly . . .'

I don't finish the sentence. I meant to finish with 'according to the rules of war.'

And then I end like this: 'Hopefully you will see something from me in the future.'

It has been an honour.

I look just like what you would expect from a soldier who has no idea how the enemy will treat him. I look scared to – and of – death. Because I am. I look just like what you would expect from a soldier who has no idea how the enemy will treat him. I look scared to – and of – death because I have good reason to be so. The Russians and their Ukrainian traitor proxies are waiting for me. I have been posting images and videos of the battle of Mariu-pol for the past weeks to the tens of thousands of people who follow me on my Twitter and Instagram accounts. The Russians know all about that because they have been goading me, calling me a liar, a creator of fake news, a war criminal. I have a sickening feeling that I know exactly what they will do to me once I've been captured. They will torture me until I break. And then?

I send one last message to my mum: 'i love you'.

As I make my way towards the rear of the bunker entrance there are about thirty to forty Ukrainian Marines standing around trying to contact loved ones. I go down the steps and walk to the bunker toilets, which stink of urine. Lazy people in need of a piss, me too, use the hole in the ground leading to the overflowing septic tank. For one last time, I delete everything on my phone. I throw it on the floor and bash the screen as hard as I can. I then snap it in half until the inner workings fall out and smash the internal storage so it can't be recovered. After that's done I throw it into the septic tank and use a pole I find near by to push it to the bottom.

Outside, one of the officers is sitting on a chair amidst the wreckage of the broken steelworks, drinking cham-pagne like he's in a fancy nightclub. I decide to go over to him. He feels as defeated as I do. He knows what's coming, we make some small talk and then I ask if I could get a drink. I take the bottle, it isn't anything grand, but it's gonna be my last time as a free man drinking alcohol. Fuck it! I take a swig, maybe two or three, then I joke: 'I hope there are no MPs' – Military Police – 'around.'

No one laughs.

Opposite me on another bunk is Boyko. He was in mortars before he transferred to the logistical company as a driver. The day before, he had been injured by shrapnel in his left leg but not too badly.

'I am scared,' he says. There is a rattle in his voice.

'That's OK,' I tell him, 'I'm scared too.'

'I want to shoot myself.'

I have a go at reassuring him. Everything will be OK, I say: 'It's gonna be hard, but remember you will go home, we have Russian prisoners too, and they aren't ISIS who kill every prisoner. You will be exchanged,' I promise him.

I am making it up. Deep down, I'm utterly afraid, more afraid than I have ever been, in my whole life.

Where to start? Listening to my great-grandfather's stories about D-Day? Fighting with the Kurds against Islamic State in Syria?

Or when the big war started on February 24th, 2022, and my battalion, the Ukrainian Marines, were ever so very close to the front line as the Russian army punched west from Donetsk to the port of Mariupol. We were driven backwards, day after day, until we hunkered down in the Illich steelworks. In six weeks, thanks to a constant onslaught of Russian artillery, tank fire and bombs, it's become a vast steel coffin, an echoing and clanging city of the dead and the dead-to-come.

By the way, the plant was named from the Russian Revolution after the second name of Vladimir Ilyich Lenin until 2016 when Ukraine's 'decommunization' laws were passed. The Ukrainians now call it the 'Illich' plant after a not so famous Ukrainian metallurgist, Zot Illich Nekrasov, so they didn't have to change the signs that much. The locals nicknamed it 'The Plant Named After Not-That-Illich', just a small example of the wicked Ukrainian sense of humour and why I fell headlong in love with the country and its people.

I risked my life for Ukraine and now I may well die for it.

Our commander has been on the radio, talking to his Russian oppo, and the details have been agreed. There's a catch in my throat as we leave our weapons behind and walk out of the Illich steelworks into the fresh air. It's seven o'clock in the morning. For weeks we have got used to the crump of incoming Russian artillery. But today, because they know we're going to surrender, it's quiet, creepily so. In the distance, I can just about make out the faint rumble of the battle for the Azovstal steelworks. It's cold, grey, overcast, a dismal morning.

The steelworks is so big that we don't walk to the surrender point but catch the bus. Well, not a bus exactly, but one of our army lorries working as a shuttle. After so many days hiding underground, in the dank murk of the bunker, it feels surreal to be outside under a great big sky. Frightening, too. We drive past pipelines and chimney stacks so heavily hit by artillery that they look as though they have been gnawed at by a plague of giant rats. There is nothing whole for as far as the eye can see. That goes for the roads too. After ten minutes banging around in the back of the lorry, we arrive at a railway line. We are slap bang in the middle of no man's land. Ahead of us is an iron footbridge over the railway line and down on the other side of the tracks the land is controlled by the Russians. As we jump off the lorry, we raise our hands over our heads in the classic surrender pose. It's just like being in a film.

Just by the bridge lies the alternative to surrender. One of our boys, a driver in his late twenties, had gone out on a final ammunition run but his Soviet-era vehicle got ambushed. On the ground, about fifteen metres from me, lies his corpse. This guy always wore a *telnyashka* T-shirt, favoured by Soviet Marines and their successors, Russian and Ukrainian alike. It's a classic, horizontal blue and white stripes shouting out 'marine!' The enemy have wrapped his T-shirt over his face, I suppose to give him in death some dignity.

We climb up the steps of the railway bridge and then down the other side where we are greeted, in a manner of speaking, by an armed Russian soldier wearing a green balaclava. Thirty metres away are two more Russians, covering him. We have no weapons; they are armed to the teeth. But they seem to be professional. They bark out orders but there is no shooting. I look around for the International Red Cross but I don't see them. Clearly, they haven't been told about this gig. I am patted down by a Russian soldier with OMON written on his uniform, not the army proper but Russian interior ministry troops. Once they've checked that we have no weapons on us, the abuse starts. It's just verbal, to begin with, they call us 'pederas' or 'peda', Russian slang for paedophile or pederast which also, to them, conveys faggot or queer. They tell us to 'fucking move it' and we get on a bus. It's rather banal and, to be honest, a bit of a let-down. I was expecting something more dramatic. Where's Hollywood when you want it? What's so strange is that there are only a few of them – OK, they're armed – but we outnumber them so we could conceivably capture the bus. But we all know our lines are too far away. If we make a run for it, we'll be dog meat soon enough.

The bus travels east for about twenty minutes, then we tumble out and are led to an old Soviet collective farm warehouse. That's when I clock new soldiers, wearing shoddier, out-of-date uniforms, some of them mismatched. At the sight of this pirate crew, not proper soldiers, my mouth goes dry. Some of them sport flashes with three initials: DNR. This stands for Донецкая Народная Республика, Russian for the so-called Donetsk People's Republic. The 'DPR' is as much a country as Disneyland. Only instead of Mickey and Minnie Mouse they have psychos.

Lots of them.

These guys are from Donetsk, the biggest city in Donetsk county or oblast, in the most eastern and most Russian-speaking part of Ukraine. They have been fighting against Ukraine and with Russia since Putin sent his soldiers, minus their identifying army unit badges, across the border in February and March 2014 at the same time as the invaders snatched Crimea and the neighbouring oblast of Luhansk. So is the DPR for real? Well, yes and no. It's hard to get this dark nonsense across, but in English terms it would be like Russia invading Southend and then creating an Essex

People's Republic to legitimize the invasion – after the fact. Before 2014, most people in Donetsk oblast supported Ukraine. Before the Russians turned up, they hit the streets, waving blue and yellow flags. Then the killing started. Kyiv is full of refugees from Donetsk, city and oblast. What's left is a vicious little joke of a puppet state. The people pulling the strings all have Moscow accents, but the Ukrainian quislings who fight for it have the terrifying fanaticism of people trying to prove their loyalty to someone else who isn't that convinced, in this case, Greater Russia. So if you are a Ukrainian soldier who has just surrendered to the Russian army, bumping into the guys from the DPR is not good. To me, they are all too real.

And then the softening up begins. For eleven hours we are forced, on pain of being beaten, to stand with our head against a wall, our hands held behind our backs, or else. Try it for five minutes. It's pretty painful. For eleven hours it's torture – and a cunning one at that. We are given no food, no water. And the only toilets we can use are two buckets. Very soon, the place stinks to high heaven.

Then there's a commotion, shouting, people being called to the front to show their documents. I work out what they're doing. It's like the bit in *Harry Potter* where they bring out the sorting hat. At some point one of the DPR guards, forbidding in his black balaclava, comes towards me. From his swagger I guess he's some kind of lowly officer, a junior lieutenant or perhaps a senior sergeant. He barks at me, demanding my documents. Let's call him 'Sergeant Blue'. I give him my military ID first, then my passport. It's in a case with a Ukrainian trident on the cover, so at first glance it suggests it's going to hold, similarly, a Ukrainian passport. When he opens the passport, he stares at it, moronically. Then at me. Then back at the passport. After a long, long time, he gets that what he's looking at is not what he's supposed to be looking at.

In Russian, Sergeant Blue asks: 'Where are you from?'

'Great Britain,' says I.

He punches me square on the nose. I guess that would put me in Slytherin. To say it goes downhill from now on would be something of an understatement.

My time inside gets darker and darker. Towards the end, it becomes black. For as long as I live, I will never, ever forget the thump, thump, thump of the truncheon against the helpless soldier in the next cell along, how his screams softened to mews, then silence, then the prisoners banging on the door, yelling for the guards. In that place, in that time, no one ever dared do that. Unless . . .

When the medic finally deigned to arrive, she was able to carry out her professional duty. That is, she declared him dead. It must be horrible to see someone murdered. But to hear someone being murdered in the next cell, and to be utterly helpless to prevent it, well, I would not wish that on my worst enemy.

That killing was perhaps the lowest point of my time in captivity. But there were plenty more.

One thousand and some miles to the west my mum, Ang – she spells it like that but it's pronounced Ange, she's from Newark-on-Trent, not Myanmar – is hanging out with my sister Shannon and her little boys Cole and Kane at

Funtopia in Grantham. They're having a whale of a time, which is great because life has been tough for Shannon and Cole, five years old, and Kane, three. Kane is very poorly, born with life-limiting epilepsy. He's registered blind, is fed through tubes, and spends a lot of time in hospital on oxygen. But on this day Kane is in his adapted buggy, loving life. The people at Funtopia, which is essentially a travelling show featuring bouncy castles, kids' play areas and face-painting, do special days for autistic kids. Ang works as a carer for autistic adults, who can be difficult, so for her, Shannon and the boys to have a laugh all together without a worry is precious for them.

Until, that is, a video of me pops up on the family chat on WhatsApp. It's been put out by my DPR captors on the Russian social network, Telegram, and you can clearly see my tattoo, 'Happy Days', on my forearm. I look like I'm having anything but. They've beaten me blue and black, black and blue, there's a deep red scar running down my forehead where they smashed my face with a truncheon, my right eye is half-closed, and there's a vivid bruise on my cheek. My hands are cuffed, my left arm masking my right hand that has swollen so massively after I used it to protect the back of my head while they were clobbering me.

They have done something to me you can't see in the video, but it's broken my resistance.

Later, my mum tells me what happened when she saw the video: 'My legs buckled and I hit the floor, my hands to my face. Then I started to hyperventilate. I couldn't talk, couldn't breathe.' My sister Shannon recalls: 'I didn't know what had happened. I thought the worst, that they had killed you.'

Ang takes up the story: 'I couldn't walk, so Shannon had to half-carry me to the car, pushing Kane's buggy with little Cole following on, not having any idea why his nanny is so upset and why the Funtopia has to stop.'

They're torturing me. But the worst thing of all is they are torturing my family too: my mum, my sister, her little boys, my younger brother Nathan too. This is only the start of a dark game, a game that we don't know we're playing, a game the rules of which we have no idea, a game of death and, maybe, life, my life. The game is about trading human flesh. The more they put pressure on my family, the more they win.

On one side, there is me, a soldier beaten half to death, and there's my family, good, ordinary Nottinghamshire folk with more than enough troubles of their own; and on the other side, moving behind the thugs who are working me over, there's someone in the shadows, someone dark and evil.

His name is Vladimir Putin and this is my story of what it was like to be his prisoner.

## Chapter Two

# The Sinkhole of Death

I blame my great-granddad Tom. He had a very old-fashioned sense of being, a quiet, understated man, around eighty-seven years of age when he told me what he had got up to during the Second World War. For a seven-year-old boy, it was ever so very exciting. Like me, he got himself captured by the enemy. But unlike me, he managed to escape. He was in the Sherwood Foresters, the famous Nottinghamshire county regiment that can trace its history all the way back to Robin Hood and his Merry Men. Well, kind of . . .

Tom was barely a lad when he joined up and was sent to Norway to hold back the Nazi invasion of that country in 1940. The battle of Narvik in the north was a disaster from the get-go. British ships were sunk by the German navy, meaning that the Foresters were put ashore with very little in the way of ammunition and supplies. Even in late spring the snow was thick on the ground, but they didn't have skis or snowshoes. Very soon, the Nazis had taken Narvik, forcing my great-grandfather and his mates to run for their lives to the safety of neutral Sweden.

After a time, the warm weather arrived and Tom talked to the Norwegian resistance movement who promised him that they could smuggle him back through Nazi-occupied Norway to a fishing village. He made it through the shadow-lands, dodging Nazi checkpoints, hiding in people's lofts, and having more adventures than you could throw a stick at. Eventually, his Norwegian pals got him to a fishing boat and he hid below deck until land slipped away. After sloshing around in the sea for a week, he was back in Blighty. The British army recognized that he was a soldier with a lot of gumption, so they moved him from the Foresters into the Commandos. With that unit, he took part in the disastrous Dieppe Raid in August 1942 when half of the 6,000 British, Canadian and Allied troops were killed, wounded or captured and the remaining raiders left with their tail between their legs. Still, lessons were learned in preparation for the big one, D-Day. Sure enough, my great-grandad Tom was there, on Sword Beach. His unit fought alongside or was part of Lord Lovat's Commandos – remember, I was only seven at the time and may not have got all the details right – and fought all the way to Pegasus Bridge. This was a critical battle because it stopped the chances of a successful Nazi counter-attack. And, what's more, Lord Lovat's Scottish piper galvanized the British troops.

My great-grandfather's war stories had a powerful effect on me, so perhaps it's no surprise I ended up doing a twenty-first-century version of what he did. To be honest, he was a far better soldier than me, yet I think a little bit of him would have been proud that I ended up fighting Islamic State and the Russian army. Different from the Nazis, sure, but not that different.

I was born in Nottingham but grew up in Newark-on-Trent. I was a bit rubbish at school. I don't know what happened, exactly, but I was a troubled kid and never buckled down to the academic grind or anything like it. I was both dyslexic and suffered from dyscalculia, which is fancy talk for number blindness.

One of my teachers predicted: 'You're going to end up in prison.' And about that she was absolutely right. Full marks to her.

I left school with hardly any qualifications, but my mum says that I was always bright. Mum would say that though, wouldn't she?

The one thing that really helped me settle down and become a little more mature was boxing. I'm a big bloke and can look after myself. But what I enjoyed was the discipline of boxing, of having to train, to eat properly, to get fit, so that you were properly ready – both physically and mentally – for a fight. I was 20 stone when I got into it, pretty fat for my height, and I got down to 14 stone. That felt good. Before I started boxing I used to get super-aggressive, very easily. But because of boxing it takes a lot to make me lash out. And another thing, I liked the honour of the sport. Yes, I know, there are all sorts of dodgy characters involved in the higher reaches of the game, but at my level it helped me make the big turn from a boy to a grown man. Listen, I don't want to oversell myself. I was never a Muhammad Ali. But I won my first fight on a technical knockout and when I did that, I felt something rare, a bit of pride in myself. I was looking forward to my second fight, but at the last moment the planned opponent couldn't make it and so he was replaced with a new bloke. One of my friends came up to me and said: 'Oh, this guy's semi-professional.'

And I went: 'What?'

So I get into the ring and this guy is built like a brick shithouse. I'm like: 'Fuck!'

Literally within ten seconds I was knocked out. I never fought in a ring again. Still, boxing helped me come out of my shell.

I fancied becoming a detective. I have a good memory, almost photographic sometimes, and – call me a fool – I like to think I know the difference between right and wrong. I never saw myself as becoming a new Sherlock Holmes, setting up rooms in Baker Street and all that carrying on, but I could imagine becoming a cop, helping ordinary people who had been the victims of crime.

Having missed out at school, I found the 'university of the internet' fascinating, often disturbing and troubling, but also raw and compelling. I went online and realized that I was left-wing but no believer in the power or the inherent goodness of the state. I believed in freedom. That made me a libertarian. My suspicion of state power made me an anarchist. I spent hour after hour scurrying down rabbit holes. Two great foreign stories grabbed my attention and held it throughout this time: first, the anti-regime protests in Ukraine in 2014, where ordinary people opposed to the pro-Kremlin president were being brutalized by riot police. Second, the war between the Kurds in Syria and Islamic State or ISIS.

I watched videos of what the terror group did to its captives: dumping a cage full of Syrian army soldiers, loyal to the dictator Bashar al-Assad, in water for five minutes so they all drowned, froth bubbling from their mouths; throwing men they accused of being gay from high buildings; decapitating westerners.

Then came the massacre of Sinjar. This happened when ISIS attacked the town of Sinjar which was the home of the Yazidi community. These are people who have lived in the Middle East for centuries but do not follow Islam or Christianity or Judaism but their own god. Hundreds of Yazidi men who refused to convert to Islam were massacred; Yazidi women were raped and forced into slavery, as were their children. I remember there was a report on the TV showing a journalist in one of the helicopters overlooking thousands of Yazidis on a mountain top desperate to escape. It was incredibly moving. The rescuers were doing their best, but they were overwhelmed by the huge numbers. They were having to leave all these other people behind because there was no space on board. That was the point when I said to myself, 'Why is no one doing anything about this?'

Eventually I saw a news article about Western volunteers who were going out to fight ISIS and I thought to myself, 'I can sit here, complain about it and be miserable, or I can at least go and do something, to stand up for my beliefs, to support these people.'

My mum didn't believe me at first, but I kept telling her 'I'm doing this.' I absolutely made sure she was clear that I was not going there to join ISIS but to help the Kurds. So she came round a bit. Obviously, she didn't want me to go, but she accepted it was my choice.

I went online, found a Kurdish Facebook group that assisted foreign fighters, and booked a flight out to the Middle East so that I could do my bit to help defeat these monsters. My plan was to fly to northern Iraq and then team up with the YPG, Kurdish for the People's Defence Units, who were taking the war to ISIS across the border in Syria. I was told the YPG would smuggle me across the border from Iraq to Syria where I would receive some training and then go to the front line. I was deadly serious about what I was doing but it's always good to look on the bright side of life, so I booked a ticket on April 1st, April Fool's Day, 2015. I turned up at London's Gatwick airport to fly to Sulaymaniyah in northern Iraq. But Special Branch had other ideas.

They stopped me at the gate, took me to one side and asked me some questions. They were professional, courteous, not at all heavy and rather good. I'd read on the internet that something like this would happen and so had prepared myself. My cover story was that I was going to go backpacking around northern Iraq and then cross the border, legally, into Turkey. 'So where are your hotel bookings for Turkey?' asked one of the policemen, reasonably. There was something about the simplicity of the question that floored me.

'Actually, I made that bit up,' I told them. 'I'm going to help the Kurds fight Islamic State.'

I'm pretty sure they had suspected that all along. They checked out what I knew about Islamic State and I think that their major concern was whether I might be a secret Islamic State sympathizer. To be fair, the cops figured out that I was sincere in wanting to help the Kurds and fight Islamic State. In a good-natured way, they warned me that Britain had no real clout where the war was taking place, and that if I got captured, they could do very little about it. I told them that I was fully aware of the dangers but I was determined to do my bit. They then let me go about my business and I boarded the plane, buckled in and, as it took off, wondered whether I would ever see old England again.

I landed in Sulaymaniyah at six o'clock in the morning, but my YPG contact, who was meant to take me to the Kurdish safe house for volunteer fighters, never showed up. I was stuck in northern Iraq with no plan and no internet. But then I managed to get some wifi from the airport and contacted the guy, who gave me an address. I hailed a taxi and got an attack of nerves because the cab had plastic sheeting on the seats as if the driver knew that a lot of blood was going to get spilt. It really looked just like the kind of cab in a Mafia movie when they're about to kill someone.

The abattoir cab pulled up in front of a two-storey house in the centre of the city. The memory of what Special Branch had warned me about at Gatwick kept on going round and round in my head. I plucked up the courage to get out of the taxi, went up to the house, and there I met the contact who I should have encountered at the airport.

He took me upstairs and, to be honest with you, I was pretty terrified because I had no idea whether this place was part of YPG, or was it ISIS?

Climbing those stairs took, it felt like, for ever. Eventually, we got to the top and I saw the distinctive YPG flag, a yellow triangle with a red star emblazoned on it. Snoozing on sofas and in sleeping bags on the floor were a bunch of westerners. One guy was up: 'G'day mate.' Jamie's Aussie accent was fair dinkum.

I breathed a sigh of relief. We stepped out on to the balcony and had a smoke. Below us the traffic hooted and weaved. Jamie filled me in on what to expect: maybe a week or two of waiting before crossing the border from Iraq to Syria, a fair bit of chaos on the other side, but the war with ISIS was all too real.

We stayed there for three days and then were driven to the mountains in the north-west corner of Iraq. To the west, down on the plains, was the Tigris river and beyond it, Syria. We arrived at around midnight at a shepherd's hut built into the side of the mountain, so in keeping with the ground that you would never spot it from above.

The Kurds are a great people, the biggest national community in the world without their own country. They are split four ways between Turkey, Iraq, Iran and Syria, and in all four countries they are treated like dirt. That said, divisions inside the Kurdish leadership makes everything worse. When I was there, the Peshmerga – the Kurdish warriors in Iraq who kept Saddam Hussein at bay when he was in power in Baghdad – were under pressure to curb the activities of their cousins in the YPG in Syria. The deal was that the Peshmerga would not let the YPG and its volunteer fighters like me cross the border into Syria, legally. But if we scampered across in the middle of the night, they wouldn't be that bothered.

In the morning the view from the hut was extraordinarily beautiful: plunging green valleys lined with trees, to the north snow-capped mountains shimmering in the spring sun, the air clean and cool. Like Scotland, without the kilts. Here, the Kurdish fighters wore traditional dress: khaki baggy trousers just like MC Hammer's, a big fat belt where they would hang their ammo and grenades, and a blouson jacket. Breakfast could not have been better in a five-star hotel: olives, a really smooth cheese, freshly baked naan bread – the guerrillas had their own bakery – and jam and honey.

It was beautiful but it was boring. We were not allowed to use our phones because our hosts were afraid of cross-border raids by the Turkish air force, who had been fighting the Kurdish guerrillas active in Turkey, the PKK. It would have been annoying to get bombed by the Turks by mistake, but life passed pretty slowly in the mountains. There were about ten of us westerners. I used to hang out a lot with a Norwegian bloke called Helge and a Croatian, Ivan.

After three weeks, we moved, walking for seven hours under cover of darkness. It started to rain and there was a terrible thunderstorm, so we got soaked to the skin as the lightning lit up the mountains and the thunder rolled. At one point we tumbled down into a muddy ditch and, being a big guy, probably the heaviest man in the unit, I couldn't get out of it. I had to call out for the others to stop and haul me out.

The rain stopped as we arrived at the Tigris river. The spring thaw meant that the river was full, high against the banks. Suddenly the moon came out and you could see the far bank, but also the vicious speed of the current. The Kurds inflated a dinghy which was going to ferry us across. I didn't fancy my chances if it developed a puncture half-way over. Fortunately, they gave me a paddle, so I stopped worrying and worked hard for ten minutes or so until we bumped into the far bank.

I got out of the dinghy and stood on the far bank underneath the sickly moonlight, the Tigris washing past me, and thought to myself, *Crikey, I'm actually in Syria.*

The YPG ran a training academy for westerners at a base, well back from the front line, in an old Chinese oil company pumping station at a hilly place called Qaracho. We were there for two weeks, learning very basic military skills and rudimentary Kurdish. The training was a bit rubbish frankly, but I picked up a few tricks from the other guys on the course. There were ten of us westerners: Joe, a Brit from Manchester; Helge, the Norwegian guy; Ivan the Croatian; Danny, a former US Marine; and others. Around this time I picked up my Kurdish nickname, Rojhat, which means 'sunrise'.

The military training at Qaracho was in fact worse than rubbish, it was pathetic. The YPG was so short of ammunition – or we were so low a priority – that we got to fire just four rounds from a Kalashnikov or AK47, the standard Soviet sub-machine gun the Kurds used. We were firing at a target, just a piece of paper with a circle on it, and I managed to hit it three out of four times. The only other weapon we got to use was firing five rounds each from a PKM light machine gun, one with a fancy bipod. So over two weeks I fired nine rounds in all. At the time, ISIS was the richest terrorist organization on earth, selling oil from the wells it controlled back to the Assad regime in Syria. They could buy all the bullets in the world; I trained with fewer than ten.

Still, the other lads taught us some of the basics of soldiering. One of the westerners who had military experience made a dummy minefield and we had to step through it, looking out for mines and IEDs – improvised explosive devices. Commonly, ISIS would booby-trap homes with grenades triggered by fine wire. So we learnt to look out for freshly dug earth – a telltale sign of an anti-personnel mine – and flimsy bits of wire.

After the end of the two weeks, we were split up and sent to different units. With Helge the Norwegian guy and Ivan the Croat, I was sent to Tel Hamees, a small town in the sticks that had recently been taken from ISIS. This part of Syria is nothing like the Sahara Desert you see in the *Beau Geste* films. The land is poor, the soil gritty, barren. Few trees thrive, but you do get gnarled shrubs here and there, nibbled by goats.

Our unit was on the front line but it was very quiet. On the roof of the house where our unit was based, there was a DShK, a heavy Russian 12mm machine gun on a tripod. ISIS were three or four kilometres away across a vast, empty brown field. Once or twice a week they shot at us and we shot back. We got bored very quickly.

At times it felt like a game. We were watching ISIS and they were watching us. At night we switched on floodlights that lit up no man's land like it was day. We also had night-vision binoculars so that we could see them in the distance moving around. Halfway across, slap in the middle of the big brown field that separated us, was a house and one time, Helge, Ivan and I went out to it. It was pitch-black apart from a night sky full of stars and cold. Syria was far colder than I had even imagined it would be. One of us flashed a torch by accident at the enemy and one of them flashed a torch back. The ISIS guy and us started flashing our torches back and forth just like a bunch of kids.

It wasn't beautiful but it was ultra-boring. We'd come to Syria to fight, not play night-light peep-bo. The thing that caused us to act was news of a big YPG military operation up north, where Syria borders Turkey, pushing ISIS west towards the base at Raqqah. The three of us, Helge, Ivan and I, became agitated and went back to Qaracho and implored the commander to send us to where the action was. The commander grinned to himself: he liked our style.

After a fair bit of faffing around, we were sent west towards the active front line. One of our party was an amazing Canadian woman, Hanna Bohman, nicknamed Tiger Sun, a former model who had left her job as a sales clerk in Vancouver to join the Kurdish women's defence force, the YPJ. Like me, she had made her way to Iraq, then Syria to fight with the Kurds because she was frustrated by the inaction of Western governments.

Unlike most parts of the Arab world, the Kurds treat women as equals and I'd come across loads of Kurdish women fighters armed to the teeth. Hanna and I became good friends and I loved to hear her fiery talk. She preferred to call ISIS by its name in Arabic, 'Daesh'. Hanna loved to be rude about them, telling an Australian newspaper: 'They're not some giant, holy juggernaut of ultimate damnation for unbelievers. They're just a bunch of filthy, mouth-breathing, knuckle-dragging pigs who run away at the first sign of resistance. Really nothing more than a thorn in the side.'

On the road west towards the city of Tell Abyad, a city still under ISIS control, we came across two corpses lying by a motorbike. They had started to rot in the heat and were covered by a swarm of flies gorging on their blood. They were the first corpses I had ever seen.

When we reached the outskirts of Tell Abyad, ISIS were on the far side of an irrigation canal, less than a kilometre from our position. Soon the sky was rent with the pop-pop-pop of heavy machine-gun fire. There seemed to be no way on earth that we could take the city. But then Danger Mouse turned up. It was the craziest war machine I have ever seen, ever, a home-made armoured personnel carrier, knocked up in a Kurdish garage where some bright spark had soldered iron plates on to a bulldozer. We piled into the back of Danger Mouse and rolled west, our hearts in our mouths, listening to the clatter-clatter of bullets hitting the ironmongery that was keeping us alive.

I can remember looking at Helge and Ivan and thinking, *This is it, we're getting what we wanted.* The racket from the bullets smashing into our armour was deafening, but we were getting closer and closer to the canal. In another hundred metres, less, I saw the driver of Danger Mouse stare through the slit in the ironwork ahead of him and gulp. And then he hit reverse, fast. He'd seen an ISIS guy train a rocket-propelled grenade (RPG) on us. If that thing had fired, we would have been dog meat. We dropped back to our position, hearts pumping. Then our Kurdish commander got on the phone and called Uncle Sam. The US air force were running missions, bombing ISIS when the YPG asked for help. The very real danger came from a false map reading, when instead of bombing Islamic State, the Americans might kill us all.

So it was with a certain grim stoicism that we heard the fighter jets fly overhead and watched a bomb fall, exactly one kilometre ahead of us, on the ISIS position on the berm or eastern bank of the irrigation canal.

You could feel the earth move through your boots. With binoculars, we watched one poor bastard stagger around in the smoke. I guess he was suffering from a traumatic brain injury and his body, in spasm, was just jerking around before he collapsed. After the air strike, the YPG called in their own heavy metal, an ancient Soviet T-55 tank, designed in the 1950s, and a Soviet-built MT-LB armoured personnel carrier. Both would have been captured from the Syrian army or ISIS. We piled in the back of the MT-LB and headed towards the canal. This time we got right up to its western bank but could go no further because the bridge was down.

We hunkered down as dusk started to fall. Ahead of us,

a field was on fire after the bomb. I was hungry – we hadn't eaten properly for days – and there was a lovely smell of barbecued meat from the other side of the canal. I stayed up for four hours on guard duty, shivering in the cold, driven mad by the aroma from across the canal, until another westerner took over and I could catch a little sleep.

At sunrise, around six o'clock in the morning, we pushed forward. Although the bridge had been broken in two, it was possible to clamber across the wreckage on foot and make it to the other bank. Just on the other side was a corpse, smouldering. That had been the source of the barbecue smell. I was 18 stone when I went to Syria and I left weighing 15 stone. That was one of the reasons I lost my appetite.

The American killing machine had done its job. Further down the road there was another corpse, or rather, bits of a body completely dismembered, his limbs blown off, his torso unrecognizable. I had no idea where his head might have been. Then, next to a massive crater in which you could have hidden a double-decker bus was another guy, his body perfectly intact. We didn't know for sure but we suspected he had been killed by the air pressure from the bomb. We checked his body and rucksack. His first-aid kit was poor, very rudimentary. I did feel sorry for them as human beings; this second guy, intact, whole, both eerily undamaged but very dead, most of all. I remember thinking, *This kid could have been at university*. Instead, his cold eyes were staring, unseeing, at the sky.

We walked into the city of Tell Abyad, the June heat rising to 32 degrees Celsius: hot. Just as we reached it, we were greeted by a sniper, the bullet hissing through the air above our heads. The place was a ghost town, utterly deserted, but the electricity was still on thanks to it being so close to the Turkish border. Hungry and thirsty, I burgled an empty house, found a fridge full of goodies and two huge barrels of fresh water, chlorinated. Towards the evening we pushed into the centre where we came across a roundabout boasting an iron cage where ISIS would put their captives on display, a little reminder that pacifism and Islamic State aren't good bedfellows.

The cage was empty, ISIS had gone, and we had won a battle. Soldiers of the Free Syrian Army, the FSA, had rocked up, coming from the south, and it was great to greet these brothers in arms. From the empty city, people started to emerge, blinking in the dusk, enjoying the first spell of freedom for far too long. Pretty soon they were moving from lamp post to lamp post, tearing down the black flags of ISIS. My pals and I had liberated a city from the most evil, best-resourced terrorists on the planet, and that felt pretty cool.

Hanna said her goodbyes. She had been fighting with the Kurds for months and the food was so grim she was in a bad way, physically, suffering from malnutrition. Not long after I met her, she had to go home to recover and recharge her batteries. After a couple of months, she was back in Syria. I admired the raw courage of this brave Canadian.

Two weeks later, we were driving south with a different unit, heading an hour away from Tell Abyad to a town where we could buy supplies. We had hitched a ride with a YPG tank transporter lorry. Some way along the journey, the driver asked us if we wanted to see the ISIS sinkhole, it wasn't far off our route.

After climbing through a barren landscape, the lorry came to a stop. There was a great fissure in the earth and at the bottom was a deep sinkhole filled with water. Floating face down in the water were corpses, helpless victims of Islamic State. You could feel the aura from it, something dark, evil in the atmosphere. We were only ordinary grunts, no one special, but we understood that something wicked had happened here.

This was the moment when I truly realized that what I was fighting against was a thing of evil.

Back in Newark, Mum was at work looking after autistic adults when two plain-clothes detectives from Nottinghamshire Police called at her home, asking for her. It's just a former council house on an estate. Nothing posh. When Mum left off work to return home to meet them, the two cops told her that they wanted to look around my bedroom. They removed my PC tower, laptops and my boxing gumshield to take a DNA sample. One of the cops was rude to Ang, according to her recollection, telling her that I would end up in an orange jumpsuit being executed by ISIS.

Mum being Mum, she made a formal complaint as to how she was spoken to, and word came back that the officer had been dealt with. Not long after, a woman police officer got in touch to say that she was from the anti-terror team and wanted to come and introduce herself. When she arrived with a couple of other officers, she also had a search warrant. They looked around, found nothing untoward, and not long after my stuff was returned.

I get that the cops were worried that I might be a secret sympathizer for Islamic State. But I wasn't and there was an abundance of proof of that. They had heard that from my own mouth at Gatwick. And they could see what I was posting online while fighting with the Kurds.

The great powers of the Western world were not doing enough to fight the evil of ISIS. And they weren't giving the Kurds the wherewithal to fight their battles for them – because fighting ISIS was our fight, was the fight of anyone who cares anything at all about freedom and democracy and common decency. So it was down to volunteer fighters like us to help the Kurds. But it is one thing to risk your own life to fight ISIS. It's quite another for the cops back home to raid your mum's home.

That took the biscuit.

## CHAPTER THREE

# Bombed by the Americans

The single most frightening weapon in the arsenal of ISIS was the car bomb or, in the military jargon we used, the VBIED – Vehicle-Borne Improvised Explosive Device. There was good reason for us to fear it. After we had liberated Tell Abyad we had pushed south to defend a village that was in no man's land. They put me on guard duty at a roadblock. To be honest, after a while it becomes pretty boring, opening and closing boots, or trunks as they call them in American English, checking out local farmers and tradespeople as they went about their ordinary lives. The tedium of running a checkpoint was lessened by chatting to a gang of sweet Kurdish kids who hung out on the corner by the roadblock. I was pleased when my spell was over and I was just putting my feet up in the guardhouse, two doors away from our checkpoint, when the checkpoint was hit by a car bomb. The crater was huge because ISIS liked to pack as much explosive into these vehicles as possible. The Kurdish guard who had taken over from me lost his right foot, the kids I had seen playing on the corner had gone. I feared they must have been killed. The vehicle that had carried the bomb was now a twisted mass of scalded metal and burnt rubber. That night, as I tried to get to sleep, time and time again the image of the moment the bomb went off super-imposed itself on the stars emblazoned across the night sky. In my darkest moments, I still wonder what happened to those poor kids playing on the corner. Had they managed to survive? Or did they get vaporized?

Once car-bombed, never forgotten. However, I later found out that being car-bombed wasn't the worst thing that can happen to you in a war, not by a long chalk.

By October 2015, ISIS was on the back foot, under pressure in Iraq and going backwards in Syria thanks to the Kurds, the Free Syrian Army and American firepower. But they always seemed to have tons of explosives, pick-up trucks and crazy suicide bombers willing to get blown sky high in the name of religion.

After Tell Abyad I had joined a new unit with the YPG, which was aiming to push ISIS away from the long border with Iraq. Danny, the former US Marine, was a couple of years older than me. He knew what he was doing, he was great company, and I felt good hanging out with him. One anxiety I had was that most of our Kurdish fighters, des-pite being tremendous people, had little idea about basic battlefield first aid. Fixing a tourniquet to stem a bleeding artery could save a life. And a leg. Former soldiers who had trained with Western armies knew their battlefield medic stuff and I always preferred it when they were part of a unit I was fighting with.

In October 2015 our unit, in Kurdish called the Tabour

Sehid Roj, was given a mission, to capture ISIS-held Al-Hawl which lay on the road between the two last remaining ISIS strongholds, Mosul in Iraq and Raqqa in Syria. Our commanders had worked out that the best way of taking Al-Hawl was not from Syria but from Iraq, and then looping back and coming at the enemy from an unexpected direction. So we headed east, with Mount Sinjar across the frontier looming in the distance. Sinjar was the home of the poor Yazidi people who had been treated so cruelly by ISIS the year before. Now the boot was on the other foot. For this operation, our Toyota Hilux pick-up travelled in a huge YPG convoy of some sixty vehicles, kicking up dust as far as the eye could see. We even had a couple of T-55 tanks and armoured personnel carriers with us, in case things got nasty.

The collapse of both the Syrian and Iraqi regimes meant that we headed into the Wild West of north-eastern Syria and north-western Iraq. There were no border formalities, no queues, no stamps in our passports. We just barrelled across the border into Iraq, our crossing celebrated by the Iraqi Peshmerga waving and firing celebratory gunfire into the sky. Despite the political friction between the Syrian Kurds, the YPG, and the Iraqi Kurds in Peshmerga, they seemed bloody delighted to see us.

We rocked up at a staging post in the scrub at the base of Mount Sinjar and hung around for two days, waiting for the weather to clear. War is chaos. But lousy weather always makes it worse. Mud is the enemy of movement. Syria gets a surprising amount of rain in the autumn and winter.

A good soldier travels light. I had my PKM light machine

gun to lug around, so my own personal kit was austere: a spare belt of 300 rounds for the PKM, engine oil and a cloth to clean it, two grenades, binoculars. For me: a change of clothes, toothbrush, toothpaste, wet wipes and, I'm ashamed to write this, no books.

Once the skies had cleared, we were on the move again. The day was sunny with no rain clouds in sight, so we cleaned our kit and I made sure my PKM light machine gun was good to go. We piled into our Hilux and headed back west towards the Syrian border, final destination Al-Hawl. All morning we made good progress, pushing through empty Iraqi villages that had been smashed to bits by US air strikes. ISIS faced a constant threat from the skies, plus a separate Kurdish push from the north-west, and were surprised when we rocked up, coming out of the east. Occasionally, a call came over the radio ordering us to stop while our scouts spied out the land ahead. Then, after a pause, we would get a call to proceed.

Finally, we got a call that the enemy were in the next village along, just two kilometres from our current position. They would have seen our dust cloud from miles away, so the element of surprise was lost. We unloaded from the Hilux, checked our kit again – you check it out of habit, you check it out of neurosis, you check it because there is nothing else to do – and then we were told we would be pushing on in one of the Kurds' very few armoured personnel carriers, a Soviet-made BMP-1, an amphibious tracked infantry fighting vehicle. I guess they snaffled these from the Assad regime soldiers when they fled to north-eastern Syria at the start of the uprising.

Six Kurds, Danny and I walked over to the BMP, ready to be taxied to the front line. Once the doors were slammed shut, the BMP's engine was so loud you couldn't hear yourself think, let alone talk, the windows were so baked with grime you couldn't see anything, and it was unbearably hot too. Granted it was late October and the nights were seriously cold, but when it was sunny the temperature could hit 30 Celsius. We drove for around fifteen minutes, the driver feeling his way through the terrain, until we stopped and got out. Our position was dire.

'What the fuck?' The driver had dropped us in plain view of the ISIS-held village in the middle of a flat desert plain. There was nowhere for us to take cover, to conceal ourselves.

To our intense relief, we heard a second vehicle coming up. This was one of the Kurds' armoured diggers. It got to work, digging some slit trenches and building up some berms so we had somewhere to hide. We kept our eyes pinned on the village while the digger did its stuff. (But, of course, everything would have been so much less anxiety-inducing if both the armoured personnel carrier and the digger had headed for the position together.) I set up my PKM facing the village and took out my binoculars to try to get a better look. The image was blurry, the distance too great. Through the heat mirage I saw figures wobble and fizzle, then I made them out a little more clearly. They were running from building to building until, suddenly, the image cleared and I could make out about fifteen fighters running directly across the open plain towards us.

Another Kurdish unit, to our left, were closer to the

enemy and they let rip with everything they had and then some. The ISIS fighters were too far away for us to engage. If we did, we would just be wasting ammo. I switched back to scoping out the village through my binoculars.

Uh-oh. I caught a fleeting glimpse of something big and white and monstrous driving between the buildings of the village. 'I see a car,' I shouted out to Danny and gave him the directions as I tried to follow it, disappearing and reappearing as it drove, dangerously fast, masked by buildings for much of the time. Next time I saw it was not good news.

'VBIED!' I shouted to Danny, 'VBIED! It's coming straight for us.' Danny clocked it too and readied himself in his position. Through the binoculars I could see that ISIS had copied the Kurdish trick of soldering steel plates to a regular vehicle so the thing coming at us looked like an albino armadillo on steroids. We were both sickeningly aware that there was very little we could do to stop it. To knock out an armoured vehicle – even a home-made one – you needed either a rocket-propelled grenade or a heavy machine gun and we had neither. Just like London buses, the Kurdish heavy-weapons trucks were nowhere to be seen when you really wanted one.

I kept track of the suicidal armadillo through the binocs, updating Danny as he looked on. Our hastily dug defences would be useless if the car bomb got close. The VBIED got closer and closer until it was only a kilometre away from us, and then as I was following it with my eyes it disappeared into dead ground.

It's hard to get across just how scary this was. A suicide

bomber in an armoured vehicle had been driving directly towards us and then he had vanished. The hollow in the lie of the land where he had disappeared was hidden from view. We had no way of knowing where he had gone. At any moment he could pop up again. Time treacled by. We sat staring across the plain at the dead ground for five minutes. Ten. Fifteen. Twenty. What the fuck? Had we imagined the armadillo?

Then the heavy-weapons truck arrived and drove over to the unit on our left that was still engaging the group of ISIS fighters who had come from the village. The enemy were trying to withdraw back to the village, so we got the command to start moving to their position to assist and began running across the desert plain to the little hill they sat atop. By the time we reached them the gunfight was over. The ISIS fighters were either dead or playing dead.

Still, there was no sight of the VBIED.

An air strike hit the village, now only a kilometre from our position. I felt the bomb land, through my boots. As a human being, I feel sympathy for anyone who is at the wrong end of a bomb. But as a soldier, the air strike was great for us. It made our lives much easier.

The light was darkening, dusk was gathering. The plan was for us to pass the night out on the plain and enter the village the next morning. We took turns doing guard duty, the night eerily quiet after the day's excitement. At sunrise we packed up and readied ourselves for the attack on the village. The BMP turned up and we piled in again, once again deafened and sightless. But this was only a short hop. The driver stopped about 500 metres from the village, dropped us off so we could find a bit of cover, then he drove the BMP back to pick up another group of Kurdish fighters. Together, we started walking towards the village and came to the top of a small valley where we saw the ghost VBIED. Only now did we see the explanation for the mystery of the day before. The driver had been moving so fast he had driven into a sunken ditch and got bogged down in the mud. Not being able to get a tow, he must have sneaked away in the night, his tail between his suicide-bomber legs. Close up, the armadillo VBIED was a fantastical thing, a great white box of steel plates over the engine of what must originally have been a big pick-up truck, plates on the sides and the back, plates on chains protecting the tyres, providing easy access if there was a puncture, and a thick, bulletproof windscreen. In the back of the armadillo there were four large steel drums packed with explosives. Had the driver not hit the ditch, we would have been blown to kingdom come.

We pushed further on into the village, listening to every sound, pausing at every street corner, waiting for an ambush, expecting the worst. The town was deserted, houses locked up and shuttered, no civilians to be seen. Finally, we reached a house where it was clear from the rubbish of war – spent ammo rounds, propaganda leaflets, remains of leftover food, still fresh – that this had been the local ISIS HQ. We hung out here and waited for the Kurdish units to turn up. Soon enough they started pouring in from all directions. I have to say I did a very comical double-take when I spotted the white armadillo suicide-bomb vehicle trundle towards me. But it was piled high with

YPG Kurds doing their thing, so I suppressed my panic. It turned out that the YPG had their very own bomb-disposal unit and they had defused the VBIED, so now the armadillo was the latest toy in the Kurdish military arsenal. To the Kurds who defused that monster, respect. I had been carrying around a small pocket camcorder to film weird stuff, so I whipped it out and made a short video of the albino armadillo for YouTube.

As we continued pushing towards the Syrian border we saw the long trench and berm that had been the old border line, broken up every now and then by long-abandoned guard towers. This crossing from Iraq into Syria was the easiest illegal border crossing I have ever made. Once again, we shot through the border with no nonsense about anyone checking our passports.

Ahead the desert plain stretched out, bleak and flat under a burning sun. We followed the line of the border on the Syrian side, pushing south-west as fast as the road would allow, only slowing down when we approached a guard post which might or might not hold a stay-behind ISIS suicide unit. The first one? Empty. It once housed soldiers loyal to the tyrant Bashar al-Assad. They had run away a long time ago.

We called a halt at a bigger guard post or small fort on a bluff commanding the plains below. It was on the outskirts of Al-Khatuniyah, the last town before Al-Hawl – both were still controlled by ISIS. As we set up, we noticed that around the position there were some old Assad regime trenches and berms. Danny and I took note of possible fighting positions while our Kurdish guys got themselves organized. It wouldn't take long for ISIS to clock that their neighbourhood had just gone downhill. Danny spotted a car in the far distance, on the Iraqi side of the border, going up the side of the mountain range that ended with Mount Sinjar. The area was still mostly controlled by ISIS and had yet to still be fully liberated. Danny and I took our binocs out and observed what looked like ISIS fighters walking up the side of the mountain range. A short while later we heard a muffled boom from that direction and then half a minute later a mortar round landed about fifty metres away, behind our position. The boom we had heard was ISIS firing their mortar at us. Danny and I scurried to our little fighting holes we had previously identified and hunkered down. Every time we heard that boom we hit the deck. Our Kurdish pals didn't bother. Their contempt for ISIS knew no bounds; besides, ISIS was notoriously rubbish at precise artillery fire. The key thing with firing mortars is sustained fire while the gunners 'bracket' the target. Bracketing is a process of firing and spotting where the mortar lands until you hit the target. If the first mortar lands 100 yards too short – the opening bracket, if you like – you fiddle with the angle of the mortar so that its range is extended by, according to an educated guess, 100 yards further on. Often, the mortar will overshoot by, say, 50 yards – the far bracket. Do a second fiddle and the third strike should be on target.

But if the firing is not nigh-on continuous, you can't get your bracketing done. Every time we heard the boom we would duck. To be fair, they got one lucky shot in. It landed around twenty metres from Danny's foxhole. Close, but no cigar.

After a time, the booms stopped and Danny and I decided to go see what there was for dinner. We had been out in the field for two weeks now and supplies were getting low. On offer, as per usual, was tea, lashings of it, naan bread, some pots of jam and what we called 'Mystery Meat', which was similar to Spam but somehow even more revolting. You could lose a lot of weight on the YPG diet.

The whole time the sky was full of the US-led coalition F-16 fighter jets circling above us. From time to time, their bombs would fall behind us, to the east on ISIS positions held in Iraq, and in front of us, to the west, on ISIS-held towns in Syria. Each time the bombs fell I felt the same bitter-sweet contrast of emotions: glad that there would be fewer ISIS fighters to deal with, sorry for the poor human flesh that was getting fried.

After a wretched dinner of Mystery Meat, Danny and I explored one of the empty buildings in the fort area. For some reason, it gave off very strong echoes as if we were in a cave, so like kids we started mucking about, singing songs from movies and hymns, laughing at hearing our voices amplified naturally. We returned to the house where our digs were. I didn't have a sleeping bag. The Kurds would arrange mattresses and blankets. Just before dropping off to sleep, I checked when my guard duty was: from 3 a.m. to 6 a.m., the graveyard shift. I was woken by the guard supervisor who nudged me and said 'Heval Rojhat tu niha nobedar î' – Kurdish for 'Friend Rojhat, you're on guard now.'

At the changeover, the previous guard told me that everything was good. I could hear airplanes in the sky. Distant booms and flashes of brilliant light in the west told me that US fighters were bombing Al-Khatuniyah and, further off, Al-Hawl.

Dawn in the Syrian desert is a thing to behold. There's something about the hard gritty surface of the land that captures and reflects light. The sky to the east went from anthracite black to deep purple to a burning scarlet to a brilliant orange as the sun rose. The thing that made the hairs on the back of my neck stand up was that sunrise is also one of the favourite times for ISIS to launch a surprise attack. So I was both awestruck at the natural beauty all around me and terrified of missing any sign of the advancing enemy. Guard duty sounds banal and it so very often is. But knowing that if you fall asleep and ISIS comes along, they could slit the throats of not just me but all my comrades – well, the fear of that kept me well and truly awake.

At 6 a.m. the guy who came to replace me turned up, so I headed back to our base to see if there was a fire going to make some tea and get some food down me. It was November 4th and, as I have said, our food supply after two weeks on campaign was becoming monotonous. I went to the back of our Hilux and had a look around for any food that might have been overlooked. Bingo! I managed to get lucky and find three cans of spiced tuna. Never mind caviar, this was, compared to eating Mystery Meat, sheer luxury. I took the tuna along with some naan bread and made my way to the fire next to one of the buildings, took out my knife to pierce the can and placed it around the coals of the fire to heat it up.

The best thing about Kurdistan was that tea was ever abundant. The Kurds made damn sure that no matter what was going on there was always a brew on the go. The sun was climbing in the sky — it would have been roughly around 7 a.m. — and the night's cold was beginning to slip away with the early morning shadows. I walked over to Danny to see what he was up to and started chatting some of our usual chit-chat to pass the time. As we were enjoying our natter, four YPG pick-ups arrived. Two were just troop carriers, the third carried our unit's heavy machine gun, the DShK, and the fourth carried our sabotage unit. To my irritation, the trucks all parked closely together, making them a sitting duck for a lucky ISIS artillery shell.

The Kurds began to fire the DShK heavy machine gun at the enemy. A boom from the direction of the rising sun warned us that the ISIS mortar unit stashed away somewhere on the Sinjar mountain range had been woken up and was now going about its business. Danny and I walked over to our foxholes and sat around them, not inside, registering our lack of serious concern. ISIS played the same amateur artillery game as they had done the day before, firing shells every quarter of an hour. Every single one flew over our heads and landed in the desert behind us.

Even so, the Kurds, by parking all four pick-ups in the same spot and firing the DShK from the exact same place, were not being professional, and I vividly remember telling Danny that, adding: 'This hanging out in a bunch is rubbish. They're not going to learn until something bad happens.'

ISIS started shooting back at our position with their DShK. But the distance was too far and their aiming was way off, so Danny and I just stayed around my foxhole, chewing the fat. Deniz, our commander, walked past saying 'Hevala Rojhat, do you want to film the Americans bomb Daesh?' – the insulting term for ISIS in Arabic. Word had spread amongst the Kurds about my pocket camcorder. Deniz was a good commander and I respected him, but I politely said no, adding that it would be foolish to join the big crowd of people at our firing position. All it would take, I told him, was one well-placed round and that could kill or maim a lot of people in one fell swoop. Deniz left us and we waited for the Americans to do their stuff. Once again, I felt that bitter-sweet paradox, of wanting the Yanks to blow ISIS to bits and also understanding that to be bombed is a terrible thing.

Ten minutes passed as the fighter jets painted contrails hither and yonder against the blue sky. We were getting impatient. Danny said: 'What's going on with this air strike? Are they just flying around up there or what?'

The sound of a jet flying low towards us meant nothing to us, just running in to take out the ISIS position on the Sinjar range. Suddenly Danny noted a pressure change in the air and pushed forward, pulling me down on top of him in the foxhole, yelling 'Get down!' Then the air got very dark as dirt blasted by the first bomb smacked into our eyes and ears. The second bomb raised a second dirt-fest, showering us with the gritty desert soil.

'Is this artillery?' I shouted to Danny, my hearing nigh-on deafened.

'No, it's the F-16,' he replied.

A third bomb fell, shaking the ground in a truly, un-imaginably sickening way. My ears were ringing with an almighty clanging, as if my poor head was the bell being clattered by a hammer inside some great belfry.

We pressed ourselves deeper into the foxhole and then Danny, who is far more religious than me, started yelling: 'Yea, though I walk through the valley of the shadow of death, I will fear no evil: for thou art with me.'

For me, I had accepted that I was about to die.

A fourth bomb, closer than before, spewed dirt into our mouths, noses, eyes and ears.

'I love you, bro!' I yelled to Danny.

A fifth bomb: the worst yet because it hit one of the pick-ups, just fifteen metres from my foxhole, a vehicle loaded with ammunition, bullets and grenades. As mentioned, we call it cooking, when ammo in the intense furnace of a bomb blast ignites of its own accord. The effect is incredibly frightening. The earth rocked again and again as grenades exploded and bullets started firing any which way. The car horn of one of our vehicles was beep-beeping, my ears were still clanging, but somehow through all of it came a new sound: that of people screaming in agony.

Still pinned down by the cooking ammo, I shouted to Danny: 'We need to move to see who is still alive!'

There was something else on my mind, too. One of the tactics ISIS would use when something bad like this hap-pened was to launch a fast counter-attack to finish off the people left alive in the confusion. Sometimes, I'd heard, the defenders would be forced to beat a hasty retreat. One of our friends had got injured in a similar fuck-up, but he had been abandoned in the hurry to retreat. Luckily, he managed to crawl back to Kurdish positions through the night.

Danny nodded, went first over the berm, and I followed next. Suddenly a fresh batch of ammo started to cook, so I had to hit cover without my PKM. We pushed round the side of the berms until we got to a small concrete bunker where we saw some of our team taking shelter, waiting for the ammunition to finish cooking off. Farrashin was one of the younger Kurdish women fighters in our unit and something of a good-luck talisman for us all. Danny and I treated her like a younger sister, and we were both delighted that she had not been hit and was very much alive.

I remember two hideous sets of sounds: the screams of the injured as they lay dying; the boom of grenades and the hiss of bullets as they cooked. To help the injured at that moment you risked being killed, and that would do no one any good.

Then the F-16 came back and everyone hit the dirt, all over again. The panic, now, was deep inside me as we ran to some deeper trenches at the rear of our position. As the F-16 circled, I was immobilized by agonizing panic. We were afraid to stay where we were; we were afraid to move.

Then we heard the BMP grunting up the bluff from behind us. We kind of knew that our commanders must have got word to the Americans that there had been a terrible mistake.

Later we discovered what happened. The Kurdish officer responsible for communications with the Americans had blundered. They had asked him what were the coordinates of the ISIS position so that they could bomb them. Instead, the fool had given them ours.

It seemed safe to check on the wounded and our kit. I ran over to where our pick-up trucks had been. They had been shredded. As I tried to check the guard post, one of our RPG rockets went off, sizzling past my head. I returned to my foxhole and retrieved my PKM, only to find a bullet – from the cooking – had gone clean through the belt-feed drum.

As I looked around, I saw what was left of some of my comrades who had been alive just twenty minutes before.

Bits and pieces of flesh littering the ground, dark red patches staining the earth, getting darker by the second.

## CHAPTER FOUR

# Hello Ukraine

Being bombed by the Americans led to panic attacks so severe that sometimes I would black out. It could only take the sound of a jet engine in the sky and I would lose consciousness, all thanks to a wretched mistake by our own side. There is something all the more terrible about what the military call 'blue on blue'. It's part of the stupidity of war. When I realized what had happened I had started screaming at the communications officer. And then I began to cry.

Yes, of course, the Kurds were fighting in what was too often a chaotic and absurd fashion, but that wasn't solely their fault. The Kurds have no country to call their own, so the Western powers and their diplomats were afraid to send them the necessary equipment – tanks and guns and armoured cars – and give them the training they desperately needed, for fear of offending Baghdad, Tehran, Ankara and Damascus.

The problem was that fighting ISIS was not the number-one priority for any of the governments in Iraq, Iran,

Turkey and Syria, especially the latter. Bashar al-Assad's regime had told its people and the world that the only alternative to the Syrian state was not a new, liberal, pro-Western anti-Assad government but ISIS. To better destroy his democratic opposition, Assad came to a strange and sickening accommodation with ISIS, releasing Islamist prisoners from his jails, buying oil from wells it controlled, trading with the enemy.

So Assad's duplicity and the West's timidity and bureaucratic inertia combined to allow the dark madness of ISIS to survive – to kill anyone who stood in its way – for far longer than it should have done. Instead of fighting ISIS on the ground directly, the West fought a proxy war using the YPG to do its imperfect best. And to help them, this is where volunteer fighters like me came in.

But I had been broken by the bombs. My panic attacks were so great that I decided I needed a break from the war and should go home for a time. The moment my plane landed at London Heathrow I got a sense that I might be in a spot of bother when armed police boarded the aircraft and escorted me off in front of all the other passengers. I felt that I was being treated by the police as an ISIS fighter, not someone who had fought against it. There was a distinction but not one the police seemed to have grasped. I was taken in a police car from Heathrow to Nottingham Bridewell custody centre where they held me for two days. The cell I slept in on my first night back in England was clean and tidy, but it was not my own bed.

They questioned me for eleven hours. To be fair, the series of strategic mistakes that led to the rise of ISIS and the failure to defeat it quickly were not the fault of the individual cops from Nottinghamshire Special Branch who dealt with me. But I got cold looks, a note of condescension, a sense of 'we've got a right one, here'. Throughout my time with the YPG I had been open about what I had been doing, posting videos on to social media of our battles with ISIS. The cops did ask me some pretty stupid questions: Was I a Muslim? No. Was I planning to commit acts of terror against ISIS? No. Did I know who the PKK were? Yes, but I had fought with the YPG. The YPG was not classified as a terrorist organization by the British government. Far from it: the British fully supported the YPG's war against ISIS. But that bit had not, it seemed, trickled down to Nottinghamshire Special Branch.

Perhaps the best explanation for this dialogue of the deaf was a question of focus. Or focuses. The Special Branch officers looked at the world through the lens of limiting terror attacks in Britain: terror attacks by ISIS sympathizers. But they were also looking out for the possibility of someone like me committing a terror attack against ISIS fighters. My lens was quite different. I had seen on television the terrible pictures of the Yazidis desperate to get on board the helicopter at Mount Sinjar. With my own eyes I had seen the empty Yazidi villages, the cage at the roundabout, the sinkhole full of corpses. I had risked my life to fight ISIS and I found it frustrating and, frankly, a bit dim of the coppers that they did not understand the proper principles – love of freedom, democracy, common decency – that had driven me to fight ISIS.

Eventually, they let me go about my lawful business,

but they kept my passport for eight months and I had to go to my local police station three times a week to sign a document proving that I was still in the country. Not having a passport meant I had no ID, so I could not even open a bank account.

I was never charged with anything. There was never a trial. Oh, how I would have loved to have been tried by a jury! I'd have put a ton of money on a jury freeing me in five minutes flat. But the bureaucracy of state control denied me free movement and made it difficult for me to function in the twenty-first-century economy. You try organizing your life without a bank account. The state had found me guilty without due process. That's what it felt like. And to think there had been a time when I had wanted to be a police officer.

But the danger from ISIS persisted and, once I had my passport back, I returned to Syria to fight with the Kurds a second time. I had some horribly close shaves on that trip too, but this isn't the place to tell that story.

When I decided to leave Syria, I was worried that I might be arrested again on my return to England, so I spent three months teaching English to Syrian Kurds who had managed to get themselves out of Syria and through Turkey to the relative safety of Greece. When I flew home to Manchester airport from Greece I was arrested for a second time, at two o'clock in the morning. I was questioned under the Terrorism Act on suspicion of engaging 'in the preparation to fight against Daesh' and possessing 'articles for terrorist purposes in Iraq/Syria'.

Once again, I had been fighting with the YPG, which is

not deemed to be a terrorist organization. Nottingham-shire police let me go but, truth to tell, I was seriously depressed by the conduct of the British authorities towards me. I had risked my life to fight ISIS, seen terrible things, watched some of my pals reduced to scraps of flesh and red patches in the earth, and all the thanks I got was to be hounded and harassed by the people who are supposed to be responsible for upholding law and order.

I fell out of love with England.

Throughout my time in Syria, I had been following the story of Ukraine's defence against the first Russian invasion in 2014 when Vladimir Putin's soldiers, without their unit identifiers so they could, at first, be unaccountable, invaded Crimea and the two most eastern counties or oblasts, Donetsk and Luhansk. I admired the way the Ukrainians, very much the underdog, had fought the Russians to a standstill. I was still up for a challenge, so in February 2018 I rocked up in Ukraine, planning to join their army.

The snow lay thick on the ground. It was brass-monkey weather, cold to the bone, and it shocked me. I had got acclimatized to Syria and was very used to British winters – damp but mild – but the deep chill of a Ukrainian winter knocked me sideways. Yet the people were delightful, incredibly grateful to anyone who was helping them fight the Russians and seriously funny. Every conversation in Ukraine ends with a joke or a gentle piece of irony, poking fun at power and authority. I loved it and I decided to make Ukraine my new home, to settle here and make a new life.

The fastest way of becoming a Ukrainian citizen was to fight for the country, and I now knew how to fight. If I did three years of military service, I could become a citizen. Serving in the Ukrainian army fitted with my core belief, that if you wish to emigrate you must adapt your culture. I would need to give a part of myself to my new country, to show respect for Ukraine and demonstrate that I had earned the right to citizenship. I knew the money was poor in comparison to what I could get working a minimum-wage job in England but, for me, it was never about the money. Or the adventure. It was about helping people.

This isn't a history book, but I want to tell you a little bit about the history of Ukraine and how Ukrainians ended up fighting a defensive war against their much bigger neighbour, Russia.

Ukraine, not Russia, came first. Kyiv was founded as a city by Viking explorers a thousand years ago. Their longboats rocked up at the great cliff overlooking the mighty Dnipro river and the Kyiv Rus civilization was born. Rus is Norse for 'rowers'. At the time the settlement of Moscow was a dump. Conversely, Kyiv grew to become an impossibly beautiful city, the spiritual and historic home of the Eastern Orthodox Christian civilization. Wars came and went; snow fell, undated. Beginning in the fourteenth century, the city of Moscow gradually developed around the Kremlin. In the eighteenth century, Ukrainian Cossacks burnt down Moscow. But Russian power grew nevertheless and the tsars conquered an independent Ukraine. The Russian-dominated world was monstrously cruel. The people under the tsar's thumb were Slav: thought by some to be the root of the English, slave.

In 1917 the Bolsheviks, led by Vladimir Ilyich Lenin, took power in Russia. They shot the nobles but kept the slaves. The ideology was utopian but the reality anything but. Those who had shot the nobles became the new nobles. They shot anyone who didn't belong in their brave new world: Tsar Nicholas II, the tsarina, their four daughters and the tsarevich, peasants who wanted land, poets who wanted the freedom to write as they pleased. Millions were killed.

Lenin had the first of three strokes in 1922 and was gradually pushed aside, dying in 1924, as a new leader emerged from the Communist pack. Joseph Stalin was a monster. Early on during the Russian Revolution, Ukraine had tried to break free from Russia and Stalin had been humiliated by a Ukrainian army. So later he wanted his revenge. In 1933, Stalin ordered the forced collectivization of farms. The result was a catastrophe. Hunger stalked the land and Stalin's famine was crueller in Ukraine than anywhere else. They called it the Holodomor. Maybe as many as seven million Ukrainians died of starvation. No one knows exactly because no one was counting. Mothers would leave their dead babies at the base of statues to Lenin: a bleakly ironic display of gratitude to their Soviet masters.

In August 1939, Hitler and Stalin drew up the Nazi–Soviet Pact, dividing eastern Europe between the two dictatorships. Victor Serge called this the midnight in the century. But nearly two years later, in June 1941, the Nazis invaded the Soviet Union in Operation Barbarossa and the people – Russian, Ukrainian, others – fought like tigers against the Germans to defend their homes. The Soviets and the West defeated the Nazis but then the Cold War started. In the Soviet Union, life was grey and bleak. In the 1980s three catastrophes eroded Soviet power: the failure of a Communist command economy to keep up with the West's free markets; the dismal failure of the Soviet army to conquer Afghanistan; the explosion of the Chernobyl nuclear power plant in 1986. This accident happened because Soviet bosses kept design flaws in the reactor secret. In 1991 the Soviet Union imploded and every single county or oblast of Ukraine voted to become independent again.

Across the post-Soviet world, democracy struggled to slip out of the shadows. In Russia it worked, chaotically, until 1999 when Vladimir Putin, a former KGB spy, became the master of the Kremlin. From the start, he was determined to restore Russian pride – and that, to him, meant bringing an independent and democratic Ukraine back into the Russian embrace. The Russian secret state worked hard to bribe, mislead, confuse and undermine a free Ukraine. Eventually, when everything else failed, Putin sent in his army in 2014 to disrupt Ukraine's ability to join NATO and the European Union.

By 2018, when I arrived, the war in the eastern counties of Donetsk and Luhansk had stabilized into a dreary stalemate. One enormous trench system divided the two armies. The killing never stopped but it was reduced to something like three or four soldiers being killed every week or so.

It's never easy joining a foreign army. First of all, they checked me out, physically and psychologically. Back before the big war of 2022, a lot of Ukrainians used Russian as their first language. My Ukrainian was non-existent, my Russian clunky – a bit rubbish, frankly – and proving that I was sane enough to fight was a bit of a catch-22. After some pretty frustrating conversations, I passed the physical and the nutjob tests and had all the right paperwork.

Then the waiting started. The military bureaucracy in Ukraine shuffled its bottom for three months to no avail. Only then did it wake up to tell me that I had overstayed my visa. So I had to leave Ukraine, hang out in Europe for three months, then come back in September. My second attempt went a lot more smoothly. I did the medical tests all over again, proved that I was not a nutter, again, got the paperwork to show for it, and received orders to go to the gorgeous port city of Odessa on the Black Sea. From there I was to travel to Mykolaiv, a second port, a little less charming, to undergo two months of military training at the naval station. I was going to become a Ukrainian Marine.

My first day was loads better than my first days with the Kurds. When I approached the gates of the naval station, I called the gate guard and showed him my military orders, explaining in my clunking Russian that I was here for training. Eventually he got the gist and after a time a man in military camouflage gear came out to me. He was just finishing his course, spoke a bit of English, and was delighted that a westerner was joining the Ukrainian military. The naval station had been built in tsarist times and, architecturally, still held on to something of the elegance of that time in a shabby genteel kind of way.

Home for the next two months was a three-storey barracks and a pretty large one at that. My billet was on the second floor, sharing a big room with around thirty other people. As the only westerner in the gang, I felt like a new gorilla at the zoo. But, Ukraine being Ukraine, I quickly made some friends. Two stand out: Roma and Vlad, both young guys who had joined the Ukrainian Marines and, luckily, spoke English. These two poor sods had to take turns translating, or attempting to translate, all the fiddly bits of our course – technical, medical, legal – into English, and I have to thank them for their patience. The military part of the training was streets better than what we had received at the old Chinese oil company pumping station in the hills of north-eastern Syria. The Ukrainian armed forces were evolving fast but there was still a lot – too much – of Soviet bull. As new recruits we spent far too much of our time Soviet goose-stepping up and down the parade ground. Kicking your legs high like some chorus girl from the 1940s is a lot harder than it looks. Our first effort made us look like a millipede with a bad dose of diarrhoea. The good old Kurds in the YPG would have laughed their socks off at such nonsense. Every army had its own bullshit, I guess. Not being a natural ballet dancer, I found goose-stepping really hard on my feet and I struggled to see how it made me a better soldier. By this time word had got around the barracks that I had been to Syria and had fought with the Kurds who, when not fighting ISIS, were also fighting President Assad's soldiers. Assad's key military ally was, of course, Vladimir Putin, so my time in Syria had made me a little local celebrity. To this audience, being bombed by the Americans in error was kind of cool.

That didn't spare me the goose-stepping. Every night at 9 p.m. we would have to form up outside the barracks for some marching up and down the square, salute the Ukrainian flag, salute the officer on duty, salute the birds in the air. At the end of our first month we were getting pretty good at the old goose-step malarkey. We did a kind of passing-out thingy, swearing our oath to Ukraine and its people. I meant every word.

And then it was party time. After a whole month of military routine, waking at 6 a.m. and going to bed at 10 p.m., and running around like a blue-arsed fly the whole time in between, to be allowed out for a long weekend was fantastic. My problem was that I didn't have a home of my own to go to or enough cash to splash out, so I slept at the barracks. But I explored Mykolaiv with a friend, including the port which had, back in the Soviet days, been one of the most forbidden spots in the whole benighted country because that was where they built the vast majority of the Black Sea Fleet. A rather good bar with excellent shisha and kebabs was called Radioactive, taking its name from the Chernobyl nuclear power-plant disaster. In Ukraine, the sense of humour is as black as anthracite.

Come November 25th, 2018, we were well into the final weeks of training when the Russian FSB coastguard – the Kremlin's secret police have their own navy – seized two Ukrainian navy gunboats and a tugboat travelling through the Kerch Strait from the Black Sea towards Mariupol. What was so chilling about this incident was that this was the first time the Russians had openly engaged with Ukrainian forces. Before, they had pretended to be Ukrainian separatists. That evening we watched gobsmacked as the TV news showed that one of the captured Ukrainian sailors had been on our course only three weeks before. It was a bleak reminder that the war, which sometimes blew hot and sometimes cold, was all too real. Ukraine's then president, Petro Poroshenko, declared martial law. In our barracks, you could cut the tension with a knife. Roma and I did guard duty, checking that our barracks was safe. As usual, we spent our time chatting about all sorts of rubbish and having a laugh. But, at the back of our minds, we knew that the Russians meant big trouble for all of us.

After we finished our training I was sent to Dachne, just north of Odessa, to the 137th Marine Battalion. I liked the people there, but the base was in the countryside and I wanted to spend what leave I had in the city. So after spending four not very eventful months on the front line I put in a request to transfer to a unit based in Mykolaiv where, in my downtime, I could at least hang out in Radioactive.

In May 2019, Ukraine elected a new president, Volodymyr Zelenskiy, a former comic actor who, once, for a laugh, wanged his dong on a piano during a show. Well, that's what it looked like. By the way, the election was free and fair. Not the kind of thing that happens in Vladimir Putin's Russia, where any opponent who might trouble the master of the Kremlin faces an unhappy end.

Off the top of my head, I would cite the following: General Alexander Lebed, who fought in Afghanistan and arranged the peace deal that ended the first Chechen War, was a charismatic soldier loved by his men. He was the notably not bent governor of Krasnoyarsk Krai province when his helicopter fell out of the sky in 2002. Boris Nemtsov was a brilliant former physicist and a great wit, who often laughed helplessly at his own jokes. Nemtsov was appalled at the monstrous corruption of Putin's 2014 Winter Olympics in Sochi. When the Kremlin and its tame oligarchs built a road-rail link from Sochi to the ski resort in the mountains for $5 billion, Nemtsov cracked: 'It would have been cheaper to have paved this road with Louis Vuitton handbags.' Nemtsov was shot dead two hundred yards from the walls of the Kremlin in February 2015. Mikhail Kasyanov was Putin's first prime minister, from 2000 to 2004. After they fell out, Kasyanov moved to oppose Putin's strut towards authoritarianism. In 2016, Kasyanov was secretly filmed making love to a woman who was not his wife. His lover, Natasha Pelevina, considered suicide and then thought: 'Fuck Putin.' The sex kompromat destroyed Kasyanov's political career – and his chance of unhorsing his old boss. Alexei Navalny is yet another charismatic potential threat to Putin. He was poisoned with novichok and, having returned to Russia to continue his anti-corruption campaign, was found guilty in a trumped-up trial. At the time of writing, his supporters fear that he is being slowly poisoned. In Ukraine, the elections are fair. In Russia, they are nobbled, big-time.

Then there is what happens to journalists, the always flawed, cantankerous, irritating but utterly necessary guardians of democracy. In Ukraine – which is still trying to step away from the dark Soviet shadow – two journalists have been killed in the last seven years in suspicious circumstances away from the war. Pavel Sheremet was a serious critic of government corruption before he was blown up by a car bomb in Kyiv in July 2016. Kateryna Handziuk exposed police corruption in her home town of Kherson before someone threw sulphuric acid in her face in July 2018. She died from her injuries in November that year. Both of these killings happened under the previous president Poroshenko. There is no suggestion that he was personally involved in either attack. No journalists have been killed away from the war while Zelenskiy has been in office.

A total of forty-one Russian journalists have been killed while Vladimir Putin has been the master of the Kremlin. Some of these deaths may have had nothing to do with power at the top of Russia. Mind you, Putin's dark joke of a legal system provides little or no redress for the families of people who get killed crossing Russians due to their power and money. Blatantly suspicious killings of open Kremlin critics include Artyom Borovik, who was reportedly working on a story that Putin might be a paedophile when he was killed in a mysterious plane crash in March 2000. Calling someone a paedophile without strong evidence is wrong. I am not making that claim here, merely pointing out what Borovik was said to be working on when the private jet he was travelling in fell out of the sky. Sergei Yushenkov was a journalist and an MP investigating whether the Moscow apartment bombings in 1999 were, in fact, a black operation by the KGB. He was shot dead near his house in Moscow in April 2003. Yuri Shcheko-chikhin was another journalist and MP working on the same story about the apartment bombings. He was poisoned and died in July 2003, almost certainly with Polonium-210, the radioactive element that the Russian secret state used to kill former KGB spy Alexander Litvinenko in November 2006 in London. Anna Politkovskaya was poisoned, survived, and then in October 2006, shot and killed in the elevator of her block of flats in Moscow. Natasha Estemirova was abducted, shot and killed in July 2009 in Ingushetia. Both women were extraordinarily brave as they reported on the Russian army's war crimes in Chechnya. In 2018, Maksim Borodin had been investigating the losses in Syria of the Wagner Group, a bunch of mercenaries controlled by Yevgeny Prigozhin, a former convict known as 'Putin's Chef' due to his chain of restaurants and catering companies providing services to the Kremlin. One Wagner unit, based close to Borodin's home city of Yekaterinburg, had suffered heavy losses when they sought to take an oil well controlled by the Kurds. The Americans warned their Russian army opposite numbers that if the Wagnerites did not stop, they would open fire. The warning was either not passed on or not heeded. Prigozhin's mercenaries were massacred and Borodin had the story on tape, from a Wagner commander telling a grieving widow of one of the dead fighters. Then Borodin died, having 'fallen out of the window' of his fifth-storey flat. You get the drift.

To be a proper journalist in Russia, you must be aware that you may be killed.

If you, like me, stand with Ukraine, one noxious thing you get hit with on social media is that Ukrainians are mostly a bunch of Nazis. Added to which, the single most cited justification for the war from the Russian side is that Ukraine is controlled by Nazis. Yet Nazis hate Jews, and Zelenskiy is Jewish. The primary Russian basis for the conflict fails to account for this anomaly, that a bunch of Nazis would elect a Jew as their president. One can only conclude, therefore, that the reasoning for the war is dark nonsense.

The second Russian argument is that the far-right has an undue influence in Ukraine. That's not true either. Political parties need to pass a threshold of 5 per cent to get a seat in parliament and at the last election no far-right party did that. True, there are Nazis or far-right individuals in Ukraine and I've met a few, as we shall see. But that is also true of any country anywhere. It's especially true of Russia. Invading peaceful democracies, well, that's what Nazis do. Russia's private army, the Wagner Group, is named after Hitler's favourite composer – an anti-semite – for a reason. Its boss, as mentioned, is Prigozhin, but his lieutenant is Dmitry Utkin, who has SS flashes as tattoos on his neck and chest. Nazi is as Nazi does.

In late July 2019, I joined my new unit, the 1st Marine Battalion of the 36th Marine Brigade. The catch was that it was an air-assault company. At some point I would be expected to jump out of a plane. To be honest, I'm scared of heights, so I wondered how I could covertly break my big toe a-goose-stepping, but in the end it never came to that. The base was eerily empty because my fellow soldiers were either at the front or taking part in a big training exercise in the Black Sea. When they returned, I was introduced to my new commander, Lieutenant Rudenko. He was a good boss and knew his stuff, having spent time in America alongside the US Marines and completed their officer-training programme. It was also great fun to meet a fellow Brit, Daniel Ridley, originally from Croydon, who had spent four years as a private in the Princess of Wales's Royal Regiment. Dan has a gift for languages out of my ken, he was always streetwise, and he was on it, whatever the 'it' was. He reminded me, a little, of a blond 'Sarf' London version of the Spanish painter, Diego Velázquez.

Finally, we were good to go to the front, travelling nine hours by military lorry to the Donbas – the coal-mining area in the far south-east of Ukraine where the Russian army had been fighting since 2014. The Russians had taken Donetsk, the regional capital, but not the whole of the county or oblast, and the Ukrainians had pushed back so the confrontation line had settled down. We arrived at a place just east of the port of Mariupol. The place names give you a little lesson in the history of that part of Ukraine that abuts the Black Sea. The -pol ending in Mariupol and Melitopol comes from the Greek word *polis* meaning city, so Mariupol is Marytown or Mary City and Melitopol, Honeytown or Honey City. There's a ton of archaeological evidence showing that in the centuries BC the Greeks settled the northern shores of the Black Sea. Place names like Mariupol and Melitopol nail that.

From Mariupol we had a short hop north-east, a little further inland from the coast, to Pavlopil, a little village where the company HQ was located. The village itself was practically on the front line. Weirdly, ordinary civilians had remained living there, even though our trenches were only a kilometre away and a Russian army just on the other side of them. By 2019, the war had morphed into a strange phoney war: static lines, little or no movement, just the Russians shooting at us and lobbing shells over, and us firing back from time to time. The Kremlin's game from 2014 onwards had not been to take over the whole of Ukraine but simply, by occupying a chunk of the east, they knew that would prevent the country from joining NATO. The organization's charter sets out a doctrine of collective security. If one nation is attacked, all the others must defend it. That being the case, NATO cannot allow a country to join unless it has full control of its borders. And Vladimir Putin knew that.

The civilians who stayed on were poor, elderly, and set in their ways. They didn't have the money or the get-up-and-go necessary to up sticks and start a new life somewhere quieter, so they stayed in their homes where they might get killed on the off-chance. Serving this small community of civilians – and us – were two little shops that carried on functioning like there was no war going on at all.

The position in which I ended up was called 'Africa' for some unexplained reason. The only way to get to it was to hurry up the side of a field while the enemy looked on. Little craters in the ground signalled the spots where they had fired high-explosive VOG grenades from their assault rifles, specially adapted for the purpose, at us.

The position itself was on top of a hill and overlooked

five enemy posts. The trenches were deep and well engin-
eered, but the ever-present threat from drones meant
that the Ukrainian soldiers who had been there before us
had started covering them from aerial view. My great-
grandfather Tom would have known all about digging
trenches. Now his great-grandson was learning that you
had to build a top for them, too.

As ever in war, intelligence can save your life. Pretty
quickly I got to know a few of the people and soon learned
that the fighting followed a pattern which both sides
respected, kind of. There was an unwritten rule that we
didn't shoot at each other in the daytime because we and
they had work to do. However, once the sun would set
around 8 p.m. at that time of the year, the Russians would
fire pot shots at us. After a polite interval, we returned fire.
This would escalate into a skirmish until one side got bored
and the fighting would come to a stop.

One time, as dusk was falling, my sergeant, knowing
that I had been in Syria, asked me if I wanted to shoot our
RPG – rocket-propelled grenade. I was up for it. They
assigned me a spotter to watch my back and we happily
trotted downhill towards the Russians, keeping on the far
side of the treeline so they would not be able to see us
coming. A gap in the trees – this being high summer, the
foliage was thick – provided a good angle on their command bunker, only 800 metres away.

Remembering a few tricks I had picked up in Syria, I
aimed down the sights, adjusted it slightly to compensate
for the light wind, and squeezed the trigger. The rule was
the moment you fired it, you legged it, sharpish. Other

people on our side could check out where it landed. While the Russians returned fire in a sporadic kind of way, we sprinted up the treeline and raced back to our trenches. I was just chilling in the kitchen bunker when one of the guys in the observation post came in to congratulate me: 'I saw through my binocs that your rocket hit their bunker dead centre.'

I don't know whether I killed anyone but I am quietly confident that I had made my presence felt. Our nights were spent snoozing in our bunkers or being on guard duty. Our days were spent doing chores: digging deeper trenches, laying camouflage nets on the top to guard against drones, getting the shopping, doing your washing. War can be astonishingly boring. Walking back to the village was a treat. We would pop into the shop to get cigarettes, chocolate or Non Stop – a terrifyingly effective energy drink in Ukraine that makes Red Bull feel like a glass of warm milk.

Zelenskiy had been busy. During his election campaign, he had gone out of his way to extend peace feelers to the Russians. The two sides agreed to recommit to a ceasefire. This came into effect at midnight on July 28th, 2019. My position commander came to me, saying: 'From midnight tonight, we are forbidden to shoot. No matter what they do, we do not open fire.'

What?

'There is only one exception,' he added. 'If Russian soldiers are clearly advancing, then you can open fire if you strongly believe your life or that of another is threatened.' That night, my guard duty was from 11 p.m. to 1 a.m., so

I would be an eyewitness to Russia honouring the cease-fire. Or not, as the case may be.

It was a warm summer night, humid. That was grand by me because I hate the cold. My oppo for this night was Dima, a smashing Ukrainian sergeant from a reconnaissance group that was attached to us. We scurried along the trench to the most forward observation post. At 11 p.m. we did the handover from the old guard-duty shift. The night had been quiet, just a few pot shots, nothing serious. Our orders were simple: 'Don't open fire. Don't shoot back.' The ceasefire recommitment had meant that we had a new chore to do: use the trench phone to call our command HQ reporting any violations, and fill in a logbook with any violations that might occur. I flexed my writing hand.

High up on our bluff, we had the advantage over the enemy who occupied lower ground. Their positions were only 800 metres away, nicely illuminated by a fullish moon. The moon was our friend because, if they chose this night to attack, we would see them come for us from a long way away. Dima and I took turns to scope the enemy positions with our thermal night-vision sights. Doing so could be dangerous because a proper observation left you exposed to enemy snipers. The trick was to pop up at random times and places, to look fast, then duck. But that meant you might miss something. Getting the balance right was tricky; getting it wrong could mean a bullet in your eyeball. If we were lucky we could use our ancient Soviet trench periscope to hand. It allowed us to look without exposing our heads to the enemy, but the optics

were a bit rubbish so that it only worked when the moonlight was really bright.

At five minutes to midnight our old Soviet field tele-
phone rang. The phone wire ran from our position all the
way back to the command post at our rear and provided
secure communications so long as enemy reconnaissance
hadn't crept up and tapped the line. It was our company
HQ checking in on us. We replied with our hourly sitrep –
situation report – code word: 'Four. Five. Zero', in Russian,
'Четыре. Пять. Нуль', pronounced 'Chetyre. Pyat. Nul'.'
This code meant there was nothing to report. Our commander nagged us about the new rules – no shooting, no
firing back – and if anyone broke them, they would be
punished. He rang off and I put the phone down, and told
Dima that it was just HQ nagging us about the new ceasefire rules.

We waited for the minutes to tick by to midnight. Those
five minutes were eerily silent, so quiet in fact that I could
hear the factory siren from the Azovstal plant twenty minutes down the road in Mariupol.

Midnight and still not a sound. The ceasefire had gone
into effect and we sat there waiting, thinking: 'Is this it?
Would this path to peace actually work?'

Ten minutes later, the Russian army resumed normal
service, firing pot shots at our position. We called our HQ
to notify them that the enemy had broken the ceasefire. It
wasn't heavy fire but it wasn't an olive branch either. Dima
took down the book and started logging the first violation
of the new ceasefire when suddenly a bullet punched
through our largish observation slit, hissed between us and

came to a stop in the sandbags at the back, which formed a kind of table for the trench phone and our paperwork.

I studied Dima's shocked expression and said: 'Cease-fire? Blyat.' This is Russian literally for 'whore', but it's used as a more general expletive. In English used in England, you could translate what I said as 'Ceasefire? Go fuck yourself.' We called up HQ, explained that the Russians had just put a round in that had nearly killed us both, and asked permission to return fire. We were told a flat 'no' and spent the rest of the shift cursing this stupid fucking cease-fire which we were obeying and which the Russians spent trying to kill us.

'Ceasefire? Blyat.'

## CHAPTER FIVE

# In the Trenches

Officers love to play swapsies. I suppose it helps them pass the time. Just after we had properly got to know the lie of the land in our old position, we were shuffled. Our new home was in a wood overlooking a field, the Russians much closer, creepily so. The good news was they had teamed me up with Dan – the Velázquez lookalike – Ash, another Brit, and three Ukrainian lads. The other bit of good news is that I had impressed the bosses with my lucky shot with the RPG on the Russian bunker and I had been promoted from rifleman to grenadier. In terms of pay, I could now order a big doner kebab rather than a regular one.

The Russians went out of their way to wreck the cease-fire. Of course they did. One night, two weeks after the Kremlin recommitted to the plan, a Russian team infiltrated themselves into our trench system in a neighbouring position, mined the trench, and sneaked out again. The next morning when four of our guys left to continue trench maintenance, they hit a tripwire or triggered some anti-personnel mines and they were dog meat: all four dead.

Then a Russian sniper crept and crawled his way up towards our lines and took out two more of our lads. So within three or four weeks of the ceasefire, the score on our very short section of the front line was Russia 6, Ukraine 0. To us, the Kremlin's cynical message was all too clear. They were completely uninterested in peace. And Ukraine's longing for an end to the war was so strong and so honestly meant, the Russians were exploiting our weakness. As the days passed, the Russian side began to increase its shooting war. Every night we would sit on guard duty taking fire from them. To begin with, it was pot shots with their assault rifles, but it got heavier. They started to use light machine guns and even their DShK heavy machine gun. If you get hit by a round from a DShK, you won't know about it. You're dead. We would call command and ask for permission to return fire. Every time, command told us just to write it down in the logbook with the date and time.

This was a joke but not a funny one. We grew increasingly frustrated and miserable at being shot at without the ability to defend ourselves. In simple terms, it's not a nice feeling. War is like a fight in a school playground, multiplied of course a thousand times over. In either case, if you don't stand up for yourself, you're going to get clobbered.

So it was incredibly exciting when, one night, we got a call from command. They wanted me to shoot at the Russians with a fancy bit of kit. The Ukrainians had built an adaptor to the standard RPG launcher so that you could fire an 82mm mortar round from it. It was a tricky assignment. When firing a mortar round you need to shoot it high because gravity is critical to its explosive impact. The higher it goes, the bigger the bang on landing. Figuring out the correct elevation requires a lot of practice. This having been denied us – remember the ceasefire – it was down to educated guesswork. I worked out the elevation, squeezed the trigger, and then ran for cover. Who knows where it landed.

Living in a hole in the ground gets you down. After a time, you have a yearning for anything out of the ordinary. Often, that meant animals. Stray cats and dogs would turn up, abandoned by their owners or, worse, their owners had been killed. I had always hated cats. Then Jingles turned up: grey, smart, a bit of posh. I soon started to love him because he was a stubborn bastard who didn't give a damn and would go out and hunt rats and mice unlike the other cats we came across. Later, lost for a present for Diana, I thought I'd bring Jingles back home to Mykolaiv. And Jingles became part of the family.

By late October 2019 we were coming to the end of our deployment. Daft as this may sound but each battalion has its own kit in the trenches and when the battalion moves, so does the kit. So as well as soldiering, we also started to play at being removal men, packing all our stuff and spare ammunition and hand-carrying it all back to the nearest track, safe for 'soft-skinned' – that is, not armoured – vans and lorries to collect it.

Our single biggest piece of trench furniture was our

pride and joy, a wood-burning stove that kept us warm at night and boiled the water for our tea. It was a colossus of Ukrainian ironmongery, a big barrel housing the furnace with a three-foot pipe coming out of the top. This monster weighed as much as a baby elephant and nearly proved to be the death of not just me but four of us.

The walk from our trench position back to the track where our vehicles were parked was roughly 400 metres, up hill and down dale through thick woodland. But the stove was horribly difficult to carry and four of us took turns, two at a time, tag-teaming as we shifted it twenty yards or so, if that, then staggering to a halt. The bad news was that at the base of the hill there was a big gap, a wide clearing in the woods where the enemy could see these silly removal men faffing about with a baby elephant cast in iron.

The Russians must have laughed their heads off before they got to work. For the whole time we had been at the front line, navigating the gap open to enemy observation had been a worry – we always trotted along this bit faster, coming or going to the shops. We often used to joke that one day they were going to take a crack at us as we crossed it, but for some reason they never had – so far. Frankly, by this stage of the deployment, we had all become a bit complacent about it, including me.

Fool, Aslin, fool.

The weight of the wood-burner made it impossible for us to move across the gap at speed. It was so heavy we also didn't want to burden ourselves with the extra clobber of body armour. A proper flak jacket with heavy ceramic panels, front and back, and a helmet, are rubbish for removal men. I should know. Being an idiot I was also lugging my bergen – military slang for backpack – which held my spare clothes, wash kit and bits and bobs that had made living in a trench more fun. Man is a nest-building animal, so perhaps it was not that surprising just how much stuff I had accumulated.

We paused just before the gap and then Ash and I lifted the handles and started carrying the stove up the hill. Dan and Zhenya, a really cool Ukrainian guy in our unit, had gone on ahead carrying some bags. The lie of the land was like this: we were at the bottom of a big hill. Roughly one and a half kilometres away, at the top of it, was the enemy position. That is, the Russians were too far away for small-arms fire, but if a DShK heavy machine gun or an RPG opened up we would be in big trouble.

Halfway across the gap we had to stop. It was autumn but we were dripping with sweat. The long trek from our trench had already knackered us. After our breather, Ash and I picked up the handles again and just as we neared safety – the top of the treeline – there was a distant boom. But my brain didn't process it. A knife-slash in time later: BOOM!

The earth exploded ten metres to our right. I fell to the ground, the weight of my bergen making it harder to get up. Dan, ahead of us in the trees, yelled: 'Dump the bags! Run!'

I wrestled with the bergen, finally getting it off my back, clocked that Ash and Zhenya were safe, and then did a passable impression of Usain Bolt coming off the starting blocks until I made it to the relative safety of the trees. Then we legged it to an old position where we knew there were some dugouts we could hide in. As we were running we heard a second rocket, but this landed somewhere away from us, on the side of the hill.

Never has a hole in the ground been more welcoming.

'Fuck, that was close,' Dan said. 'I thought Ash and you were goners.'

In my book, there is nothing better than coming back from the dead. The Russian firing having stopped as suddenly as it started, we sat listening to the surreal quiet of the woodland, laughing ourselves silly that we were all, somehow, still alive.

But what to do about the bloody stove? It was still out there, in full view of the enemy. We faffed around a bit, reluctant to leave our lovely hole. Eventually, we nipped back to the gap, picked up our stuff and my bergen and stashed that temporarily in the treeline. Then we headed back to the stove and lifted it as fast as we dared into cover.

When we had sorted ourselves out, we bumped into a Ukrainian soldier, part of a new unit, who helped us get in touch with our command. We asked the boss whether we could return fire. Once again, the message was 'no'.

At dawn the next morning, we heaved up the stove from where we had left it and then managed to get into our vehicles on the track, and so on to our depot, without any more adventures.

These days some people are worried that wood-burning

stoves are so bad for the environment that they pose a real danger.

I should fucking say so.

Life in and out of the trenches continued. Life out of the trenches got a whole lot better when I met Diana through a dating app. She was a Ukrainian woman teaching English in Lviv. We hit it off immediately. She is funny, smart, good. And very good at mocking me. There is something about the contempt of a beautiful woman I find incredibly exciting, and Diana could often – with good reason – be extremely contemptuous of me. After we got to know each other in person, she moved from Lviv to Mykolaiv on the Black Sea where she got a job teaching English to soldiers at the naval station. We rented an apartment on the edge of the city. Our first place together was a bungalow with a little garden, all on its own. This meant that when I was home on leave, we could spend as much time as possible together. Sitting at home, sipping a brew, laughing at Diana taking the piss out of me, I was thankful that I was still alive. I could see a future for myself in Ukraine with Diana.

But the war in the east had settled down to a tedious game, a static slugging match. There were rare moments of terrifying violence and people, especially our people, were still getting killed. But my sense of excitement and adventure drained with every passing month, with every new trench dug, with every time we were commanded not to return Russian fire. Like all soldiers down the ages everywhere I began to long to do something else. I was bored with not being my own boss, bored with the bureaucracy, bored with not sleeping in my own bed. By the autumn of 2021 my plan was to finish my contract, which expired in October, and start a new career as a conflict journalist. I fancied myself as the new Ross Kemp but with more hair. It is fair to say I had learned how to survive in a war zone, more or less. I knew a little about geopolitics, and I knew a lot about being arrested by Nottinghamshire Special Branch.

To advance my ambition to become a conflict journalist I bought myself a ton of gizmos, cameras and bits and pieces, all of which boosted my platform on social media. On top of that, I was making a documentary showing the life of a soldier in the trenches in the twenty-first century and trying to build awareness of Europe's forgotten war. The more people ignored the war in the east of Ukraine, the more Vladimir Putin could get away with mass murder. I was doing well on Instagram, Twitter and YouTube, getting more and more followers, posting more and more little films and using social media to raise money for our battalion. My fundraiser hit $7,000, helping my unit buy or replace laptops the commanders used to work out mortar-fire targeting, generators for electricity so we had some light in the trenches, plus treats to raise morale: cigarettes, chocolate, energy drinks, anything that would make the guys happy living in a hole in the ground with the Russian killing machine breathing down our necks.

This made me popular with my comrades. What I didn't realize was that others were watching my presence on social media like a crocodile lurking in a waterhole.

For all my talk of becoming a war reporter, somehow I ended up signing a one-year extension to my contract. Once I had signed on for one last year, I switched out of being a classic infantry soldier into a heavy mortar unit. To explain to people outside the military, a mortar is a small bomb, commonly a foot or so long although it can be much bigger, fired from a tube supported by a bipod, all three legs, as it were, resting on a big circular flat plate. The bomb or round looks a little like a fish, streamlined head, fatter tummy reducing to a tail fin. It goes up high, higher than Everest, then tumbles down, gravity enhancing its lethal impact. When it lands on say, tarmac, the explosive in the nose cone ignites and the bomb fragments into scissors of shrapnel which whizz across the surrounding area. A piece of shrapnel the size and shape of a sycamore seed can kill; in all modern wars, artillery, and specifically mortars, kill many more soldiers than bullets fired from rifles.

Both Russia and Ukraine used 120mm Soviet-designed 'Sani' or 'Sleigh' heavy mortars. These are real monsters, weighing 500 kilograms, the tube as tall as a man, the unit so heavy it is commonly towed by a lorry. Getting range and elevation right so that the mortars could hit their target cleanly was challenging but interesting work – well, more interesting than digging trenches – and I got stuck into it.

Our new deployment started in the second week of November 2021, not too far from our old patch in Pavlopil. This time our position was pretty much due east of Mariupol, four kilometres from the Russian army. In simple terms, the moment the Russians launched a second invasion – and every day we saw fresh videos of Russian trains carrying tanks, armoured cars and big guns west, towards us – we would be some of the very first defenders to stand up to the advancing killing machine. Common sense told me to get the hell out of there, sharpish. But I had signed up for an extra year and, besides, I had committed myself to standing by Ukraine. The winter days rolled by, snow fell on our trench in droves, and the news got yet more bleak.

Mind you, we still had a laugh. One of my great friends in the marines was a fellow Brit, originally from Bedfordshire, in his late forties, funny and very fit for his age. Shaun Pinner had served as a soldier in the Royal Anglian Regiment, then left, worked on the bins or something for a bit – he called it 'waste management' – and then, like me, had got himself to Syria where he fought with the Kurds against ISIS. I met him on my second tour of Syria and from the get-go Shaun and I got on like a petrol station on fire. He was funny, really funny, so funny that he would make my ribs hurt, always up for a laugh. After my first spell in Ukraine, I caught up with Shaun and told him it was a really exciting place, so he came over, signed up with the Ukrainian Marines, and found himself a Ukrainian wife. It was almost as if Shaun was stalking me. I had joked with him: 'I bet you the moment I sign up for another year, Putin will do a second invasion.'

Call me Mystic Meg.

Our position was just four klicks – kilometres – from the zero line and eerily part of some forgotten battlefield from 2014. It had been abandoned a while back, some of the trench walls had collapsed and mother nature had come back with a vengeance. Apart from exorcizing the ghosts of the soldiers who had lived and died where we were now, we had a ton of chores to get everything shipshape, as well as addressing immediate anxieties, shielding our presence, as best we could, from Russian drones and artillery. So we spent a lot of time putting up camouflage nets and timber to mask our trench system from prying eyes. It did not take that long to clear and clean our patch.

The four-man crew in our bunker were pretty relaxed. I was on the top bunk above the lieutenant in our mortar unit, Ihor, while our sergeant, Mykola, and David, the youngest, were in the bunks on the opposite side. My Ukrainian pals seemed to have a problem with both 'Aiden' and 'Aslin', so my nickname was Johnny. Our trench was rather luxurious: we had not only a log-burning stove but electricity too, siphoned off from a line from the nearby village but backed up by the generators I had fundraised. We had company, too, three cats; an old black cat that was queen of our trench, a little grey one about six months old, and a third one that popped in and out, every now and then.

It's smart practice to put the mortar pit some way from where the soldiers sleep, so we always had a little commute to get to it. Mortar shells contain high explosives so you have to look after them properly. You cannot leave them in the sun. They may expand and crack the tube. Not good. You can't leave them out in the snow or the rain either. Rust and high explosives don't mix well. So we spent quite a lot of time putting the shells safely away and then getting them out, ready to return fire. Once again, we were under strict orders not to start anything. If attacked, we had to put up our hands and ask, 'Please, sir?' Most of the time came the answer 'no'.

Come the first week in December, things started to get interesting. Someone with a sense of humour had made our 'prepare to fire' emergency alarm into an ultra-tacky Russian pop song, 'пошла жара', pronounced poshla khara, meaning 'It's getting hot', by the Gayazov Brothers. Translated into English culture, it would be like waking up in the middle of the night to try to stop people killing people by killing the killers first to the sound of Rick Astley's 'Never Gonna Give You Up'. We clambered into our warm clothes – it being -15 degrees Celsius outside – while doing our moves to the Gayazovs beat. Command came on the line, explaining that one of our positions close to us was under attack. A Russian scout or reconnaissance unit had tried to sneak into their trench system. Thankfully, they were spotted before they were able to seriously penetrate our lines, but we had been tasked to hit the area where command thought they might be.

Our mortar pit was a tight fit and shifting mortar shells into position fast was a hell of a lot harder if you had your body armour and helmet on. So we chose not to wear them. Better be fast in and out of the mortar pit than slow. Still swaying to Russia's version of Rick Astley, I pulled my wellington boots on and ran along to the pit. David, a smart, kind and sweet Ukrainian soldier, logged the target coordinates and prepared the elevation on the sights. Ihor, our boss, came down and shouted: 'Ten rounds, four charges! OK?'

'Yes,' I yelled back.

Ten rounds means ten bombs; the charge is the thing that fires it out of the tube. The technology that drives the Soviet mortar high in the sky is pretty stone-age. You take the propellant charge, a slug of explosives wrapped in a thin cotton bag the size of a fat sausage, and wrap it around the stem of the bomb leading to the tail fin. When you drop the bomb into the tube, the belly of the bomb makes a snug fit. On pulling the trigger, the firing pin hits the detonator which ignites the charge in the tube and the massive air pressure released by the explosion forces the bomb high up into the sky. The more charges you wrap around the bomb, the higher it goes. Four charges can make the bomb travel four kilometres. Traditional artillery has a relatively flat trajectory. But because a mortar's arc has the shape of the croquet hoop, it can hit targets on the other side of a hill or pretty close to the firer; it makes a great tool for trench warfare.

We were ready.

'Load one round!' Ihor barked. None of this was routine. At this stage of the not-quite-phoney-war, we hardly ever fired anything. Hence his tension; hence ours, too.

Our mortar bombs or rounds weigh 15 kilograms each – the weight of three large sacks of potatoes – and big lad as I am, it's hard work shifting these blighters. I picked up the round and handed it to David, who dropped it gently into the tube. I was the trigger man. We waited for the command.

'Johnny: Fire!' I yanked on the rope and the mortar fired, deafening me and rattling my brain. In my great hurry to get dressed and out of our bunker to that bloody stupid Russian pop song, I had forgotten my ear defenders. It didn't help being in the enclosed space of the ammunition tunnel, built into the side of our trench system.

Ihor shouted for us to reload. Again, I pulled the trigger and continued until ten bombs had been fired. We then covered up the remaining shells to protect them from the winter frost, draped the camouflage netting back over the mortar pit, and legged it. Firing mortars is not a question of pinpoint accuracy, but the enemy get a pretty good idea of where they have come from. They can and do fire back, so it's never a great idea to hang out by a place from where mortars have just been fired, just in case.

It was freezing outside but I'll be damned if we didn't get a workout from that. I was dripping with sweat, catching my breath because shifting 150 kilograms in a minute or two in a cramped pit, your body at an angle, is a lot harder than it sounds. I chucked off my coat and shirt and dried my body with a towel. Then back to Bedfordshire – sleep – wondering if we would hear that bloody pop song again before dawn.

The next day we got some good – by which I mean well-sourced – intelligence that we had killed one Russian in the mortar-fire mission. It had been a team effort between the four of us, but this was a strange and sombre moment for me: my first confirmed kill of another human being. In Syria, such was the chaos, you never knew who had killed who because there would always be sixteen other guys shooting. When you went forward and saw a dead ISIS fighter, nobody ever knew who had got them.

Truth to tell, I didn't feel much when I learned about killing the Russian. By this point I felt pretty numb about killing and/or being killed. So many of my close friends had died in Syria: fifteen alone in the American air strike. More had died since that grim day, so that my American pal Danny and I were the only two surviving out of a group of some thirty people.

After I heard about the dead Russian, I messaged my Croatian friend Prebeg, who served in the infantry company our mortar-fire mission had supported. He had been very close to the fighting when our ten mortars hit the enemy.

'That was us: the hammer of God,' I told him. It was a bit of a joke, a bit of a brag, about the first kill of this deployment. This kind of banter is absolutely normal in wartime military culture. But I can imagine a normal civilian reading this and thinking, *Oh, Aiden, you sick, twisted soul.*

This is how the madness of war works on you. You start out hoping for an adventure, testing your courage, knowing that you are fighting for a good cause. You end up in a dark, dark place. What I didn't realize was that, for me, very soon it was going to get a whole lot darker.

## Chapter Six

# The Big War Begins

New Year's Eve 2021 was spent in our little snow-covered hole in the ground, waiting for the big war, waiting to kill or be killed. The run-up to the celebrations had been spent watching endless videos of trains loaded to the gunnels with armour and transport being moved from the far reaches of Russia and rolling west, towards us. The Kremlin was saying that was a training exercise and, as usual, it was talking rubbish. It was bleeding obvious they were preparing for an invasion, a far bigger one than in 2014. It was no longer a question of 'if' but 'when'.

The enemy was quiet, so we cooked a fancy meal – well, fancy for people who live in a hole in the ground – and watched President Zelenskiy's speech on television bidding farewell to the old and hello to the new. As soon as he was done, we switched channels and watched Mr Khuylo strut his stuff. Khuylo is both Russian and Ukrainian for dickhead, so you should be able to guess exactly who I am talking about. Nothing too interesting there, but one thing stuck in my mind, namely that Vladimir Putin said

Russia's main goal was to 'improve the welfare and quality of life for our people'.

He lies so wickedly.

The news was getting grim, grimmer than before. Open-source media – videos shot by ordinary Russians – showed that they were now moving fuel tankers, medical vehicles, air-defence kit right up to the front line. You don't do that with just an exercise in mind. It was hard not to feel gloomy. A week or so after New Year, Stuart Ramsay of Sky News paid us a visit. They foregrounded Shaun Pinner and me. After my trouble with Special Branch, I worried a little about using my real name. Obviously, the overwhelming majority of the guys filmed were Ukrainian, but Sky's logic was that the folks back home would be more interested in seeing a couple of mad British lads fighting for Ukraine. We were both in smart, arctic camo gear that looked pretty good as we walked up and down trenches covered in snow. But the camera never lies and it picked up our gloom, our sense that soon the Russians would be heading this way. After we finished the interview I remember saying to the people from Sky: 'The next time you see me I will either be dead or in captivity.'

How we laughed.

On January 27th I was granted two weeks' leave. I took the overnight bus to Mariupol, arriving around 6.30 in the morning, but I just missed Diana who had already left to teach at the naval station. The sight of a washing machine was a relief. I put all my filthy uniforms and underwear into it, pressed the button, and watched the good voodoo of the machine doing its stuff for a bit. Then I remembered that I, too, was filthy, so I had a bath. It took a tremendous effort to get out and dry myself, then I crashed in bed for most of the day.

Diana got back around four o'clock in the afternoon. We fell into bed and had a good old time. And then around eight o'clock, I threw on some clean, civvy clothes – oh, so lovely – and headed to the train station to travel to Kyiv. My grandma and younger brother, Nathan, were flying into Kyiv airport, some of the very last tourists to visit Ukraine before Mr Khuylo's 'special military operation'.

It had been four years since I last saw my grandmother. We took the overnight train and got back home to Mykolaiv in the morning. It's not one of the world's great tourist destinations but it does have some Soviet-era delights. But we all got along and had fun, and it was sweet to see that both Nan and Nathan fell in love with Ukraine. There's something really rather beautiful about the spirit of the people here.

After we said our goodbyes and they headed back home to England, I caught Covid. I didn't bother to see the medic at the base to get tested as there was no doubt about the diagnosis, and also because I was too busy being lazy at home. Nothing better, if you're a soldier, than not having to dig or lift mortar bombs all day long. I spent my second week of leave doing not very much. Well, the one thing I did get done was make Diana a bug out bag. That's soldier talk for an emergency bag if you have to get out of somewhere in a hurry. I'd also got her some body armour and a helmet from my personal stockpile of military gear. In this part of the world you need to be prepared.

The drumbeat of invasion grew louder and louder, so

insistent that it was impossible to put it out of our minds. Russia likes invading neighbours in the middle or at the end of an Olympics. Russia's invasion of Georgia in 2008 took place during the Summer Olympics in Beijing. The Kremlin's first invasion of Ukraine in 2014 took place during the Winter Olympics in Sochi. That pattern told me that as soon as the Chinese Winter Olympics were out of the way on February 20th, 2022, the Russians would start a big war against Ukraine.

On February 12th I said my goodbyes to Diana before returning to military duty and as I got into my taxi I thought to myself, bleakly, *This is probably the last time I will see her*. I had a gut feeling that going back to the front line was wrong. I felt as if I was sending myself into a situation I knew I wouldn't be able to get out of. A simple glance at the map – and the videos of Russian tanks on freight trains trundling west – told me that our brigade to the east of Mariupol would end up getting surrounded on two fronts, from the east, from Donetsk, and, through Crimea, from the south-west.

My heart felt as heavy as a mortar bomb. As I arrived at Mykolaiv bus station, I bumped into some of the other guys from my battalion who were catching the same bus. Their faces were every bit as grim as mine. As I stood there in the pre-dawn cold, waiting for a bus, last stop 'Certain Death', I was so close to leaving and heading back to the house that I had opened my phone up to check the Uber app to see how much the taxi would be. I stood transfixed, staring at the app, trying to make my mind up whether I should miss the bus and return to Diana. Every part of my brain was telling me not to go.

The bus arrived and I forced myself on to it knowing full well what was about to happen. I held my true feelings inside as my mind battled with two conflicting urges: I wanted to go home, but I feared the disgrace and shame of doing so. I knew I could be court-martialled for going AWOL – army slang for 'Absent Without Leave'. On that I was thinking of making some excuses. The best runner was that I could still be infectious from the Covid. But it was too late. The doors on the bus closed and we pulled out of the bus station.

On reflection, I think back to my dithering about getting on the 'Certain Death' bus a lot and how many other soldiers, knowing that the odds were very much against them, must have suffered on the same rack: fear of death fighting fear of shame.

At Mariupol the next morning, I was met by some journalists from the *Daily Telegraph*. As before, my message to the West was that we didn't need NATO soldiers but we did need air defence. At Pavlopil, I asked to see the medic for a Covid test. She took out the Covid test thingy and twirled it around my nostrils and joked, in her sweet but limited English, 'I just fucked your nose.'

We both fell about giggling but after a few moments I let out a deep sigh. Had I got the test done in Mykolaiv, I could have got two weeks' sick leave to spend with Diana. I headed back to my position and cracked on with what needed to be done, the days passing, the old routines kicking into play and helping me get my mojo back. Russian social media started showing their tanks and other vehicles painted with the letter 'Z'. No one had any clue what they were for sure, but common sense said these were identifiers. On the Sunday before February 24th I had gone with the lads from the company to the battalion logistics HQ point. Our side was painting identifiers too.

The big war was coming. But many good people in the Ukraine, from Zelenskiy down, couldn't really believe it was going to happen. Our lieutenant, Ihor, said: 'They do this every year.' Our sergeant, Mykola, was also sceptical. I sensed I knew what was coming and felt a little fatherly towards David, the youngest out of the four of us. I told him to make sure his stuff was packed and squared away, ready to go, because Russia was ready to invade. I believe he got it, too.

The next evening, we received orders to prepare the mortar vehicle and bring it to the position to hide it, in case we needed to make a fast exit. That decision suggested to me that the bosses were getting it. The next command was that everyone should prepare a bug bag, but stuff it only with what was truly necessary.

No wood-burners in a bug bag.

On Wednesday, February 23rd we got a new order, restricting all movement. No one was allowed to leave the position. Later that evening, a second order, to switch off all electronics and to go radio silent. I told Ihor that I was going to head to the mortar pit to prepare twenty rounds on 4 km charge. I got to work, finished my task and hit the sack, knowing that I had to get up at midnight to do my radio shift watch.

At midnight I woke up to do my shift and sat on the bed, listening for our radio. It was quiet, some non-committal grunts. I laid down and played a stupid game on my phone. But at 2 a.m. I heard the ever-so-distinctive sound of grads being fired in the distance, and then, closer by, the ominous sound of multiple impacts. Grads are a classic Soviet artillery weapon: a volley of rockets stacked in rows of tubes are fired in very quick succession from a self-propelled lorry. Back in the Second World War, they called them Stalin's Organ. More than any other piece of artillery, grads have a very distinctive sound signature. The thing is, at no time in the static trench warfare of the last three years could I remember hearing a grad. They had been banned from use under the Minsk II agreement with Russia signed in 2014. Grads were a very big sign that things were not OK.

This was it. I jumped down and woke up Ihor and told him grads were being fired. As he listened, everything went back to being quiet.

'It's nothing, Johnny,' he said. Then went back to sleep.

So, this, then, wasn't it.

The radio stayed silent. I lay in my bed listening to the grads thumping in the not too far distance before finishing my shift at 3 a.m. I woke David up to take over, told him what was happening and to get dressed so he was ready. I got dressed myself, put on my warm kit, and laid down on my bed.

For twenty minutes, nothing happened but I just couldn't get to sleep.

Then the unit laptop came to life. That fucking Russian pop song was blaring at top volume.

Ihor jumped up and shouted: 'To battle.'

Just imagine doing that to the sound of something very much like Rick Astley's 'Never Gonna Give You Up'.

Still, this *was* it. Full stop.

## Chapter Seven

# The Battle of Mariupol, Lost and Won

It got bad extraordinarily quickly. I jammed my feet into my wellington boots, ran along the tunnel that led to the opening of the trench, and stepped out into a world of noise: artillery crumps getting closer, morphing as they did so into savage crack-cracks, but what was much grimmer was the snap, crackle and pop of people shooting at each other. I hadn't heard that sound for a long time.

And to cap everything, the weather was bloody awful too. It was pissing down with rain, heavily overcast, cold. Mud and mortars don't mix. To rub it in, I slipped on the mud steps as I hurried down into the mortar pit, banging my elbow hard on something. The bottom of the pit was a sea of sludge. That made everything much harder for us because, to be accurate, the mortar base needed flat, solid earth to sit on. Instead, the base was already capsizing into the ooze. A few days before, in the rain, we had fired only a few rounds when the base started sinking. This would make it much harder to get it out if we needed to extract it in a hurry. I ran into my little rat tunnel where the bombs were kept and tore away the sheeting that was protecting them from the elements.

'Range?' I yelled to David.

He took the degrees, figured out the elevation, and yelled back: 'Four.'

Moving fast, I double-checked my bombs were all snug as a bug in a rug, prepped the detonators by removing the safety caps, and yelled: 'Ready!'

'Ten rounds: Fire! Fire!' shouted Ihor.

The mortar was set to automatic firing mode. Getting into a rhythm I swung the bombs to David who plopped them in the mortar, then came the bang.

After each round fired, my brain wobbled. I finally got to the last bomb and handed it to him before he dropped it down and we shouted: 'Finished.'

Ihor told us to conceal – drag the camo netting back over the pit – and get inside quick. As we scurried back to our bunker, we heard a deep bass drumming: grads being fired. Then the earth moved, literally, gobbets of earth spattering down from the trenches into our faces. Once inside the concrete shell of our bunker, it was hard to work out how close were the impacts. But my bunk bed was vibrating – and that didn't feel like good news.

Still, after all the agonizing and the frustration of not being able to fire back, it felt good to hurl something at the enemy. We stood, poised for fresh action, waiting for the command to go back to work, waiting, waiting. Ihor asked us how many prepared rounds we had left and I told him fifteen.

We could hear the artillery rounds crack-cracking in, we

could sense the small-arms fire getting closer by the minute but, because all our phones were switched off, we had no idea of the big picture, whether the Russians were pushing forward only in the Donbas or whether they were trying to capture Kyiv or, indeed, the whole of Ukraine. I asked Ihor if we could switch on our phones and he said yes. Before the big war, none of our mortar crew had smoked. Then, just like that, out of anxiety at what might be coming, all of us were chain-smoking, working our way through a carton of Marlboro Red that Sky News had gifted us a few weeks previously. As blue smoke coiled against the roof of our bunkers, our phones pinged like crazy. Never in my whole life have I stared in disbelief as my phone juddered with hundreds of incoming alerts. The mass of them made it impossible for me to read, to work out what the hell was going on. So I opened up Google and just typed in 'Ukraine'. The page loaded and instantly I was met with hundreds of articles with titles like 'Russia Invades Ukraine'. I clicked the first BBC link and saw that all of Ukraine was being attacked, that the Russians were landing in Odessa, that Mykolaiv was being heavily shelled. I hit Telegram to contact Diana and saw a bunch of heart-rending messages from her. One, sent at 2:43 a.m., read: 'Baby, I'm dying of anxiety. Please send me at least one word, at least a sticker as soon as possible.' It was 4:02 a.m. I replied: 'I'm good. I love you.' She then messaged me to say there was a big shoot-out at the military airfield, just a few blocks from our flat. I messaged back, telling her to pack the body armour, some clothes, our laptops, but not much else, and to move.

Then came the bad news. The whole military was on high alert and everyone – even an English-language teacher – had been ordered to report to base. She had to comply. Desperate now, I messaged Diana straight back, saying turn around, go home, get fired, the Russians are landing in Odessa. She didn't reply, so my anxiety multiplied. Again I messaged her: 'Go home! Listen GO HOME!'

The naval station was the last place where I wanted her to be. She wasn't a soldier but a civvy teaching English. I was angry and frustrated, hundreds of miles away in Donbas while the love of my life was under attack and our home was in danger of being captured. An agonizing silence fell before she messaged me to say that her boss had said to her: 'What on earth are you doing at the base? Go home.'

But for Diana it was out of the Russian frying pan into the Russian firing zone. Once she got home, the Russian assault on the military airfield went into overdrive and the whole area was peppered with artillery. I started thinking I needed to do something to save her, that I couldn't stay in Donbas, not while she was in danger. I was torn, feeling desperate. I didn't care about Donbas, all I cared about was the safety of my fiancée. She was in grave danger of being killed or, somehow worse, being captured. As someone working at a military base, she would be seen as a collaborator.

I was burning up with anxiety. I got on very well with Ihor, our lieutenant, so, after steeling myself, I reluctantly said to him: 'My fiancée is in danger in Mykolaiv.'

'If you want to go, Johnny, I won't stop you.'

The thing is that I still hadn't fully decided I was going to do it. Some people might think of me as a coward, but I was guided by the great words of G.K. Chesterton: 'The true soldier fights not because he hates what is in front of him, but because he loves what is behind him.'

Diana was in great danger. Still locked in doubt about what to do, I poked my head out of our bunker and at that very moment heard a volley of grads being launched. A few seconds later: incoming, but thankfully the salvo flew over our heads. I went back into the bunker and told the boss: 'I've changed my mind. I'm staying.'

Ihor did not say anything, but his face crinkled up into a sweet smile.

I knew that what I was staying on was most likely the path to suicide. But I just couldn't leave my Ukrainian pals in the lurch at this, the worst moment in their lives. Then the Russian pop song burst into life and we were legging it to the mortar pit or, rather, the mud-pie pit. Shifting 15-kilogram bombs when you're wading shin-deep in mud is horrible work, utterly knackering. I prepared the charges again and we got the order to fire another ten rounds. Then the training took over and we got our rhythm going. I started swinging the shells to David, and he slid them into the tube. One by one they fired off on their way to some unfortunate sod. But when David dropped the sixth bomb into the tube, nothing happened.

'Abort!' I yelled. It was our signal for when a mortar bomb doesn't go off. The commander shouted for us to get inside quickly. As we did, we came under another volley of grad rockets, but once again the Russian aim was well off. Our position was tucked away in the cleft of a valley, which made it harder for the enemy to locate us.

Or else they were very stupid.

A mortar misfire is always scary because getting a bomb out of the tube isn't child's play. The possibility is real that the charges will be detonated suddenly, killing not the enemy but us. After a bit, Lieutenant Ihor and Sergeant Mykola – the two most experienced soldiers out of the four of us – headed back to the pit to fix the problem. We were all on edge, knowing that a mistake could maim, blind or kill one or more of us. Ihor and Mykola decided that the best thing to do would be to disconnect the tube from the base plate. Then they would lift the tube upside down so the bomb could slide out. We didn't have a bomb extractor like they do in Western armies. I'd read enough about mortars to know that sliding the bomb out was a lousy idea and so I refused to stand in the pit while they carried out their plan. (Later, when I got captured by the Russians, I learnt from other mortar men that the trick is to smash the base of the tube with a sledgehammer so the bomb doesn't stick. I'd pay to see that done – but at a distance.)

As Ihor, Mykola and David began to tilt the tube, Mykola had his shoulder pressed against the tube hole when – sod's law – the bomb fired, flying out of the tube and up into the sky. The recoil jolted Mykola's shoulder, tearing his jacket but not ripping off his arm. He was deafened in his right ear, poor man, and staggered back in the mud pit, bewildered by the noise and the pain. Still, as he limped off to lick his wounds, we knew that he was the luckiest man alive.

To add to our misery, the accidental firing had buried the mortar base deep into the mud. David and I started digging it out but then our spade broke. We stood there, staring at the useless tool, the rain sluicing down from a grey-on-grey sky, our feet rotting in the cold slime, the crumps of artillery getting closer, feeling that this is how armies lose wars. At that very moment, a pick-up turned up with a brand-new mortar and there was word of more people coming to help us.

Now that it was a sump, it made sense to abandon our old, damaged mortar and move to a new mortar firing position away from our trench. The downside of that plan was that I had to shift our store of bombs too. There was a top hatch in our rat tunnel, so I lugged the bombs through that and then we started running them down the muddy field to the new firing position. We shifted around twenty bombs – that's 300 kilograms or, in old money, roughly 50 stone or two very fat men. Exhaustion piled on exhaustion. With the new mortar came some new bombs, charges and detonators. Our team was joined by a new soldier. David set the sights, the new guy loaded, and I prepared the charges. We fired off ten more rounds, but it was still raining. Whoever had been looking after the new fuses we had been sent was a fool. The top safety caps had rusted and were incredibly difficult to remove. You can still fire a bomb with a safety cap on, so I was all for that. But David was worried. We compromised on me being right.

The noise from the front line that day was incredible.

When the artillery crumps quietened for a few moments, you could hear the shrill buzz of Russian drones spying on our positions, then the thwack-thwack from the rotors of Russian attack helicopters in the distance. We got a call over the radio that a Russian helicopter, most likely a Kamov Ka-50 'Black Shark', was approaching. Luckily it didn't come our way as it could have blown apart our position.

Things were not going well, to put it mildly. You could see defeat written on our faces. Or hear it in the despairing chatter on the radio. Or the continuous crump-crump, buzz-buzz, thwack-thwack, all day long, every sound a warning that you might die at any moment.

Around four o'clock in the afternoon, we got the order to up sticks. Time was not on our side. Frantically, we shifted as many bombs and charges and detonators as we could move to our truck, but we abandoned the new mortar where it was as we didn't have enough time to run down the hill to fetch it. We went back to the old pit to try to get the old mortar out. The base plate had been damaged in the misfire, the recoil from the tube bashing a huge hole when the mortar tube had shot a round off while they tried to move it. After a lot of mud-wrestling, we got it to the truck and loaded it along with our bags. I went down into the rat tunnel and passed out some more bombs for us to take. Ihor said, 'Stop. Leave them. We don't have time.'

Then I came up with a cunning plan. In the rat tunnel there were still about fifty bombs which would make quite a bang if they went off. So while the others were loading their stuff into the truck, I ran into our bunker, opened the box of grenades, grabbed one, and then ran back to the rat tunnel. My plan was to leave a present for our Russian friends by putting a grenade with the firing pin removed beneath a ton of mortar bombs. The Russians used the same Soviet mortars as we did, so the moment they saw our treasure they would start nicking it. And then: BOOM! Unless, that is, they were careful or lucky. This sounds cruel but war is war – and it's entirely within the rules of war to try to kill as many of the enemy as possible so long as the target is military. No civilian in their right mind would go anywhere near my rat tunnel and start shifting fifty mortar bombs.

I had been trained how to use a grenade but I had never done it before in anger. To be honest, I was absolutely shitting myself, engaged in what was probably the most stupid thing I've ever done. Mortar bombs covered the floor of the rat tunnel. Kneeling down, I figured out the best place to conceal the grenade. I made a space under the bombs where it could go. This particular grenade had two safety features: you had to both release the trigger and, separately, pull out the pin. It would not go off if you just did one action. I pulled out the pin but kept my finger firmly pressed down on the trigger. I eased the grenade, trigger up, underneath the mortar bombs. With infinite care, I placed a bomb on top of my finger on top of the trigger. All I had to do, as the weight of the bomb took the strain, was pull my finger out.

If I fucked this up, I would be bad dog-meat. Even though there were a few seconds' delay on the grenade, which might have given me enough time to jump round the corner, the amount of explosives in fifty 120mm mortar bombs was enough to blow up the corner, the rest of our trench system, and most of the valley we were in.

No time to be jumpy. I slid my finger out from underneath the bomb and slowly reversed out of the rat tunnel – moving one of the other bombs might cause the whole thing to go off – and climbed up the stairs and out of the mortar pit. I told the guys not to go anywhere near the mortar bombs.

The bunker had been pretty much emptied by now, apart, that is, from the wood-burning stove. I grabbed my personal stuff and a US Marine Corps flag I had been given by American friends the previous summer. When I had told them I was going to take it to the front, they had said 'Don't let the Russians get their hands on it!' I was honour-bound to take that. I told our commander we should take our Ukrainian Marine flag with us, too, which we did.

Our pick-up was ready to go. You could hear the shooting war getting closer to our valley. Ihor asked David to fetch the two-stroke petrol we used for our chainsaw so that we could torch down the wooden stuff – the bunks, rudimentary table and chairs – in the bunker. We got the command on the radio: get out.

After three deployments we would be leaving Pavlopil for good and burning down our old home to boot. At the very last moment we remembered the cats, the strays or abandoned pussies that had kept us company in our hole in the ground for months. I went down into the bunker, calling for them – 'here, kitty, kitty' – but the racket from the war meant that they had gone into hiding in the bunker's woodwork. Fingers crossed, cats being smart, they would move once they smelt smoke.

Ihor lit the petrol and the whole bunker went up in flames. David and I jumped into the back of the truck, then Ihor asked for the grenade box and took two grenades.

'What for?' I asked.

'I'm going to blow up the mortar bombs.'

'Stop!' I roared. There were far too many bombs. He could kill us all. And, besides, I told him I had booby-trapped the place for the Russians. Ihor nodded to himself, smiled, returned the grenades to the box, and got behind the wheel of the truck.

As we climbed out of the valley, we saw a series of craters in the earth where the Russian grads had been overshooting at us. It was only seventy metres off. We had been very lucky.

As we drove south-west towards Mariupol I looked back at Pavlopil. It had taken the Russians just fifteen hours to kick us out of there.

When we first arrived at the Illich steelworks, the lights were still working, and the mobile phone network signal masts were still online, so our mobiles worked. Quite a few of the steelworkers at the plant were still lingering around, not sure what to do, not quite believing that their old life was dying in front of their very eyes. They would die, too, if they didn't run for it. But for a little while Mariupol was deceptively quiet, making the decision for people harder to judge. Sometimes it was so quiet you could pretend to yourself that there wasn't a war going on.

In the early days, Mariupol was not completely encircled, so civilians and our injured soldiers could get out and fresh supplies and Ukrainian troops could get in. The Russian killing machine was moving towards us like a giant crab, two pincers snap-snapping in our faces. On the right slowly moved the pincer from the east, from Russian-occupied Donetsk, while the second pincer, on the left, was creeping up from Crimea to the south-west.

When we were in the countryside our whole battalion of roughly six hundred men was thinly spread out, up hill and down dale, but in the steelworks we lived cheek-by-jowl, three or four storeys below ground. A direct hit by a Russian bomb would wipe us out, but the plant was so vast the odds of that happening were low, so in our favour.

Early March in Ukraine is still bitterly cold and the militarily sensible decision to kip down as far below ground as possible placed us another few degrees below zero. At night we broke up wooden pallets and set them on fire, but you can't heat six hundred men all in one go. It was freezing, hideously so, beyond words.

Ihor, our lieutenant and our lorry driver, had picked up a new weapon, an American-made 62mm mortar. The bombs were tiny compared with the rounds we used in the Sani or Sleigh Soviet-designed mortar, but the gear was extraordinarily light by comparison and far more accurate. Their range was not as good as our Soviet-designed heavy mortar, but we all sensed that, sooner or later, the Russians would get close enough. David and I made ourselves comfortable with our new toy, and then it was time to play soldier.

One of the big bosses, a major, called everyone to line up in our squads and then gave us a briefing. He asked for volunteers to work on RPGs. I decided to volunteer because, before I joined the mortar unit, my old job had been as a grenadier on RPGs and I understood them far better. My gang had no problem with this. I went to a new hangar where the RPG team were being trained. However, once there I realized I had misunderstood what was required. I knew my way around the old, heavy RPG 7, but they were using the new RPG 27, a lightweight single-use weapon. I quickly decided that I would be of better use back with the mortar gang. I explained the problem and came back to Ihor, Mykola and David, who greeted me with derisory smiles.

We sorted out the sleeping area for some senior commanders and then I sneaked off, upstairs, to try to find some ciggies. By this time the carton of Sky News cigarettes had all but run out. As I was making my way up the stairs I noticed people were glued to their phones, so the signal was still good. I switched mine off flight mode and then a torrent of messages popped up, many from pals, but the most precious from loved ones and most importantly my Diana. I messaged her to say I was fine and that we had retreated to Mariupol. The good news was that the Ukrainians had managed to push the Russians back a little, but much of Mykolaiv was still under threat from Russian artillery. I suggested that she should either take shelter in a bunker or, better still, move to her brother's place, two hours north of the city and a bit safer. But martial law was now in force and travel between cities was restricted. Diana was funny and calm, and calming, and it was a balm to listen to her voice and knowing that she was, if not safe, then less endangered than before.

I caught up with what was happening across the rest of Ukraine. Every bit of news I saw was grim, but at the same time it didn't look as bad as I thought it could have been. Up north, near the capital, Kyiv, Ukraine was definitely giving Russia a bloody nose. That felt reassuring. I grazed on the internet, trying to get a proper picture of Vladimir Putin's big war. Remember, I was just a grunt in a city so close to the Russian front lines that we were bound to get surrounded. But even I could see that the Kremlin had overreached itself. The sums of war work like this. You need more attackers than defenders. A simple ratio is three attackers to one defender. The Ukrainians had roughly 300,000 men, so the Russians needed 900,000. Instead, Putin had launched his full-scale invasion with just 200,000 soldiers. They could take a big bite out of their far smaller, far weaker neighbour. But they were not going to be able to eat up all of Ukraine. Not at all.

Looking up, I realized that, mesmerized by news of the war I was fighting in, I had been looking at my phone for two hours, more. I headed back down to the freezer to see what was up. Some of the guys were preparing Molotov cocktails, now renamed Bandera smoothies, to throw at Russian tanks. (Vyacheslav Molotov was Stalin's foreign minister, the one who signed the Nazi–Soviet Pact in 1939. Stepan Bandera was a Ukrainian who had fought both the Nazis and the Soviets.) They are home-made bombs. You fill a glass bottle with petrol and stick a wick of paper in

the top. You light the paper, throw the bottle at the tank –
or whatever – and run for it. I was pretty sure that petrol
bombs were not going to cut the mustard against the Russian army. But just the fact of doing something to register
that we were still in the fight cheered up the guys.

My feet were still fucked from spending far too long in
the mud-pie pit, the skin white and flaky from the damp
and sweat. Wet wipes are a soldier's friend. I hadn't been
able to clean my feet for days. Taking my socks off was a
great relief. I cleaned my feet with the wet wipes and put
on some new dry socks.

David rocked up and told me to shake a leg, as it were,
because we were both on guard duty for three hours. It
would be bloody cold hanging around, so I put on every
single bit of thermal gear I owned, so much so that I looked
like Michelin Man even before I stuck on my body armour
and helmet. I grabbed my rifle, found David, and had a
quick smoke before one of the guards on the shift that was
ending found us at the guard post and led us through the
steelworks to where our stag or guard duty would be. We
followed our guide, sometimes walking in the open air –
there was no moon, so it was pitch-black – sometimes
walking through the brilliantly lit plant, arc lights turning
night into magnesium-ignition day.

After a ten-minute walk, we got to the guard-duty area,
but there was no sign of the other soldier. Until, that is, I
looked up. Our guard position was the high catwalk at the
same level from where the crane-driver controlled his
machine, from just below the very ceiling of the plant, a
giddy ninety feet above ground. We started climbing a set

of steep metal stairs up to the crane-driver's eyrie. The view was extraordinary. We were at the western edge of the factory, facing the giant Russian army pincer originally coming from Crimea and the south-west but now threatening us from the north too. The sentry showed us the sights: over there was Mariupol, the lights still burning, looking bizarrely peaceful; in the distance, both to the west and east, the darkness was lit up by flashes from the artillery duel of two armies, clashing by night. To see this spectacle from so high up felt like a weird privilege, a moment that spoke to the otherness of war.

David cracked a joke about the plight we were in, how it was all 'very pizdiets' – Ukrainian and Russian slang which could delicately be translated in English as 'We're fucked.' I brought up the time when we were in our position a week before the invasion and the others were saying the Russians were just messing about, that they would never invade, and I had told him it was in fact going to happen. He grinned and replied: 'Da, pakka, da' – 'Yes, OK.'

Our graveyard shift continued. It must have been minus ten degrees, bone cold. Towards the end, we were jumping up and down to keep our blood flowing. I asked David if he had any cigarettes left and he fetched his packet out of his pocket and offered one: a true friend. Times were getting desperate and cigarettes seemed to be the only thing that kept us alert and provided some comfort. The crane catwalk was lit by floodlights so our silhouettes stood out crystal-clear. If there were any Russians out there, they could for sure see us clear as day.

As it neared three o'clock, David asked me to go back to the guard post to collect the new shift. I was up for that because the walk would warm me up. As I made my way to the bottom of the stairs, I took a glance up at the crane, towering above, and the control panels, lights still flashing, as if begging to be put back to work. To see it void of people, to know, pretty much, what was going to happen next, gave me a fit of the blues.

Halfway along to the guard post I saw two shadows walking towards me on the unlit part of the path. I readied my rifle and called out the password challenge, 'Four'. They replied: 'Two'. That made 'Six', which was the magic number. These were the two guys due to take over from us. I walked with them to the bottom of the crane steps, telling them it was quiet, with just flashes of artillery in the far distance. As we arrived, I wished them good luck and waited for David to come down. We made it back to our bit of the bunker, where I took off my body armour and warm kit and socks to give my poor feet a bit of an airing. The sleeping bag was far from warm, but I was so knackered from night after night of hardly any rest I was soon asleep.

Wake up. Guard duty, again. The single most irksome thing about being a soldier is that you have to do what you're told. It was a grisly day, driving rain, overcast. However, in the daylight we were able to look at the landscape properly for the first time: outside the perimeter of the plant lay ugly industrial suburbs and beyond that the countryside stretched far and wide; to the south-west lay the city of Mariupol and beyond that the Black Sea. To the north-west, the curls of smoke in the distance got closer during our shift. That meant the front line was coming our way, with the Russians right behind it.

The moment our stag was over, we hurried down to the kitchen to see what the jackals had left for us to pick over for breakfast.

The answer? Cold porridge. Blyat!

As ever, I had my new-found nicotine habit to fix. Everyone was out of fags. Gloom and despair. Then one pal kind of hinted with his eyes that he had one to spare. We moved to a quiet corner of the plant, where no one was looking, and he handed over the blessed cancer stick. I smoked it, slyly. But one fag wasn't going to cut it. The word was out that the city was still functioning, kind of. I still had a fair chunk of money left over from a fundraiser for a new axle for our Soviet-era minivan. A minor tragedy was that we had had to abandon the van back in Pavlopil, so I had cash to spare. I went to find one of our drivers to see if they would go to a supermarket to buy everyone cigarettes, chocolate, treats and all. I found a guy, a fellow smoker, who jumped at the chance.

That sorted, I returned to my unit only to get the short straw. In the rout from Pavlopil, all of our units had left a ton of mortar rounds behind. We now had fresh supplies of bombs, detonators and charges, but they had to be organized and then moved to various units across the steelworks. Hours passed as we unloaded, then sorted. As we did so, yet more trucks began to arrive, this time carrying the very best of Western killing technology, stuff I had never clapped eyes on before, such as British NLAWs – Next-generation Light Anti-tank Weapons – and US-made

Javelins, another kind of tank-killer. There must have been around fourteen of us, but it was still back-breaking work. The amount of ammunition we were unloading seemed to me to be enough to last for at least three months should the worst happen, that is, the coming encirclement. After around two hours of hard slog, Sergeant Mykola came over to us for a new task. This was much more like it: five lorries had gone to the local Epicentr K store – Ukraine's version of ASDA and B&Q, rolled into one – and had got the OK to empty the place. So a veritable treasure island now fell off the back of the lorries: cigarettes, pop, raw meat, dried meat, pasta, yoghurts, chocolate, cheeses, mats, sleeping bags, thermals for people who had lost their gear in the retreat, all sorts of goodies. As soon as they were unloaded, the lorries went straight back.

Traipsing up and down the stairs to secure the goodies from the store was tiring, but I managed to get out of it when our lieutenant, Ihor, told me to follow him. The officers needed a command centre and the place for that was the workers' locker room. Our job was to stack all the lockers on top of each other, freeing up enough space so that the battalion's senior officers could have some desk space for their computers and paperwork. Then it was back to unloading the loot from the superstore. While we were working, a slew of buses turned up, carrying fresh troops from Ukraine's central reserves. All of this was good for morale.

The days merged into each other: sleep, wake up, smoke, guard duty, eat, sleep, smoke. Until one day in early March we were huddled in the stairway of the bunker, sheltering from the rain, when the air was rent by a sudden burst of pressure and there was a deafening bang. They had hit the steelworks clock just by where we had been unloading the lorries.

The enemy was at the gates. Or, at least, close enough to clobber us with tank fire. It started slowly and sporadically. And then it got worse. From the moment they hit the clock tower, we could no longer freely walk around. By March 10th the word was that Mariupol was surrounded, the city cut off. You would hear rumours that there was still a corridor, a way out, but it sure didn't seem that way. We were under siege.

Virtually all the civilian steelworkers had long gone, seeking safety in the city or even daring to leave, walking out, west, parallel to the seashore. One night, walking back from a guard shift, I came across a bloke in civilian clothes who was, as the phrase goes, 'acting suspiciously'. I told you I had wanted to be a copper once. I told him to get out, but he refused. There was something odd about his behaviour, so I detained him. Two other soldiers watched him while I checked his pockets. He had two cheap phones with different Ukrainian and Russian sim cards and a Russian bank card. We brought him back to HQ and they called Ukrainian intelligence, the SBU, who came out from the city to investigate further.

Early one quiet morning in mid-March, I had done my guard duty and headed inside to go and get some kip. I took my boots off, snuggled up in my blanket and must have been in the bed for an hour when the steel emergency hatch door behind my bunk blew and a great shock-wave blasted me. Dust, grit and all sorts of crap flew in and covered me from head to toe. One of the guys ran in and stared at me because I was so covered in dirt I looked like a corpse from a movie.

'All good, Johnny?'

'For fuck's sake.' I could not have achieved better comic effect if I had tried. He started to laugh because this particular corpse was clearly very much alive and, more or less, unhurt. I got my boots on and went to find out what had happened. A Russian fighter jet had dropped a bomb close to us and the pressure burst was so powerful it had smashed open the hatch even though we were some twenty metres below ground. Nervously, I climbed up the stairs to see the damage. The bomb had pulverized the steel-works' three-storey office building, just forty metres opposite us, bringing most of it down so you could see filing cabinets and desks hanging on the edge of nothing. The bomb had hit the office car park too, blasting some cars to mangled wrecks of metal and wire, setting fire to others a little further away. A yellow bus was ablaze, its horn blaring like a great beast in pain, and thick black smoke billowed into the sky. I ran downstairs to get my body armour and helmet on, just in case the fighter bomber came back, and picked up my camera to capture the scene.

At the top of the stairs of our bunker, I hesitated. From this position I had a slight angle on the fallen office build-ing and the burning cars, but the shot would be far better if I got out into the open. Contemplating what to do, I bumped into Sasha, a soldier from another company. A little older than me and clearly with a bit more balls, Sasha walked straight out into the open to get a better look at the carnage. Following his example, I too went out and started filming the broken building and the burning metal. In Russian I asked him what had happened.

'We were sleeping nicely then the fucking Russians woke us up.'

Pithy.

Hurriedly, we ran past the burning cars to try to find the crater. The bomb had sliced through hard concrete as if it was butter, collapsing the bigger part of the office block and leaving a huge hole. Sasha, who was just shy of six foot, jumped in and stood at the bottom, and virtually disappeared. Luckily, perhaps because it was so early in the morning, no one was hurt.

By the way, our battalion HQ was set up in the deep basement of the office building, so the Russian spies knew their stuff.

Some days later, a second bomb fell on a disused part of the steelworks, some distance from our bunker – the main building was roughly a kilometre long – blasting a railway wagon on its side.

To be honest, I had still not properly recovered from being bombed by the Americans in Syria. Perhaps I never will. After Syria, the symptoms of my post-traumatic stress disorder would come and go, come and go. Immediately after being bombed four years before, I suffered panic attacks so dreadful that I would black out. The blackouts eventually stopped and by the time I moved to Ukraine I thought I had properly recovered. But now I was back in a place where being hit by enemy bombs from the air wasn't just a possibility. It had happened twice already. All I had to do was look at the crater by the blasted office or the wheels of the train wagon up in the air.

My demons were back. I tried to push back against my anxiety about being bombed as best I could and remain my normal idiot self, talking rubbish, playing practical jokes and having a laugh with my mates, but the possibility of getting blackouts again left me, in my darkest moments, sick with fear. I am the very last person to say that I was brave. But, in my experience, courage isn't a matter of having no fear. That's just stupidity. Courage is knowing that you feel fear and are doing your best, if not to conquer it, at least to get on top of it.

The sight of injured civilians did not lift the mood. Far from it. As the Russian killing machine started to capture whole sections of Mariupol, the city hospital was effectively cut off to ordinary people who lived in our part of the city, so, at wit's end, they came to us. One day, two civilians who arrived in an army pick-up caught my eye. They were an older babushka, wearing a granny-style dress, and her daughter, in her forties, in jeans and a jacket. They were so coated in blood it was as if they had been spray-painted red. I ran for my camera and filmed them being cleaned up by our medics. They explained to our doctor that they had been at home when a jet bombed them, killing their dog but, somehow, they had survived. A neighbour had dared to give them a lift to a Ukrainian checkpoint and the soldiers had driven the old woman and her daughter to our steelworks. They were not seriously hurt but, after the medics had patched them up, they were taken by car to our battalion HQ in another part of the steelworks where the facilities were less basic.

On March 16th the Russians bombed the Mariupol Theatre, frying civilians who were hiding in a deep shelter directly under it. To demonstrate that the shelter was home to civilians, the word 'ДЕТИ' – pronounced 'DYETI', meaning 'KIDS' – had been painted on the tarmac in front of the theatre in huge letters. Only the Russians have a good idea of how many innocent men, women and children they murdered that day, and they're not being open about their war crime. The most conservative estimate, of at least a dozen dead, comes from Amnesty International; the highest number, 600 corpses, was published by the American news agency, Associated Press. Some people may have managed to escape before the bomb hit, it was reported, but many had sought shelter there.

Four civilians came to our base for help: a man, two women and a young girl. They, too, were covered in blood. I got my camera and filmed them from a distance, making sure not to get in the way of our medics. Not everyone died due to the bomb blast. Some, trapped under a mountain of rubble, were buried alive. The Russians tried to say in the media that the theatre bombing was faked, that it was Ukrainians who had rigged the place to blow up. We all knew that was bullshit.

The Russians had no regard for civilian casualties, full stop. I saw evidence of this with my own eyes.

From our lookout position high above the steelworks, we had a grandstand view of the battlefield. If the night was moonlit and clear, we could see for miles. One full moon, when I was on guard duty, I saw a great volley of grad rockets being launched in our direction. Death coming your way can be an eerily beautiful sight to behold. I gazed at the starbursts of brilliant lights and then, far too late, started clattering down the stairs to save my bacon. However, nothing happened, and I slowly made my way up again. More volleys of grads were fired but, by the light of the moon, I realized they were landing amidst the big blocks of flats in the city. The Russians were deliberately targeting civilians. That is a war crime.

On another night a jet whistled overhead and, true to form, I legged it down the stairs. Again, the citizens of Mariupol, not us soldiers in the steelworks, were the target. Yet there was not one but two explosions. The first bang was softer and, thanks to my time in Syria, I knew exactly what it was. The first explosion would have burst open a few hundred feet above ground to release a cloud of cluster bombs, mini-bomblets the size of a golf ball containing hundreds of ball bearings. The effect on anything living below is lethal. Targeting a civilian area with cluster bombs is also a war crime.

On March 22nd I posted a video on YouTube telling people about the details of Russian forces hitting civilian areas: 'Since we've come to Mariupol, we're now in the outskirts defending it, just on the very outer districts. But since then, Russian forces have continued to target the civilian areas where we're not located. And I know this first hand because I've watched it. I've watched multiple grad vehicles launch their rockets into the civilian areas behind us. And this is the Russian military. So, if they're as professional as they say they are, then they would know who they're targeting, civilians, causing multiple deaths, casualties every day.' I went on to say that the civilians were 'not a part of this war', and I specifically called out the Russians for bombing the Mariupol Theatre where civilians had sought refuge: 'That entire building is now levelled.'

It turned out that some people watching these videos intended to do me harm the moment they got their hands on me.

## CHAPTER EIGHT

# Defeated

Netflix kept me sane. Well, sane-ish. We still had a tiny bit of phone service. There was a dark moment when my Netflix subscription was about to lapse and I could not resolve the problem from Ukraine for some stupid reason. I started pounding my younger brother, Nathan, with messages to renew my sub or else I would box his ears. Being a good lad, he fixed it. *Rick and Morty* was my favourite. It's a science-fiction comedy featuring an alcoholic sociopath grandfather and his slightly wet grandson going on adventures in granddad's flying saucer through multiple universes. It was the perfect distraction from the irritating proximity of the Russian killing machine.

Even late in the siege, our petrol-fired generators gave us power so we could charge our phones. In my downtime, night after night, I became obsessed with two films. The first was Quentin Tarantino's *Inglourious Basterds*, which I got to know word for word in both English and Russian. The second film was *Dunkirk*. I got a kick out of it because what was happening here in Mariupol happened to the

British army in Dunkirk, the difference being that no one was coming to rescue us.

Then the phone-mast signal died. As far as communicating with the world was concerned, we were dead.

On April 1st, April Fool's Day, I awoke around six o'clock for my morning guard duty. My body clock had adjusted to the weird hours we had to keep, so I could switch on and off as easily as an electric light.

Boots. Warm kit. Coffee.

The mountain of supplies we had looted from the superstore some weeks back had reduced to a molehill. Food, treats, cigarettes were all in short supply. I had swiped a packet of coffee when the superstore bonanza came in and had hoarded it. Keeping something of your own to yourself made all the other troubles more bearable, somehow.

There was a section of our bunker called the Old Soviet Decontamination Area. I was never quite sure what or who got decontaminated, but we used it as a smoking room, and somewhere you made your early-morning coffee. Kettle on the boil, I went up to some of the guys, pitifully asking any of them if they had a smoke to spare. Nothing doing but no harm done.

Our guard duty these days wasn't on top of the crane catwalk but manning the HQ radio, making sure that all messages in and out were logged, and that routine sitreps from outlying units were delivered. Whenever a Russian fighter jet got close or bombed near by, the units dotted across the steelworks site had to call in to say that they were all OK. As the sight of Russian fighters became all too common, rather too many radio operators got bored with this chore. Part of me enjoyed giving them some shit if they didn't report in. Of course, if we were busy, then I wouldn't bother. Command is all about do as I say; not as I do.

One of my regular buddies on radio guard duty was Misha. After a brief half an hour of downtime, he would come by my bunk to check that I was ready for our shift. My ritual was to make two coffees, one for me, one for my Thermos flask.

To work the radio we had to be at ground level, so we were always kitted up with a flak jacket and helmet. Thankfully, our position was covered with a roof so Russian drones were not able to clock us. At a little past six o'clock in the morning, the sun slowly crept into the sky. This shift was generally quiet, the Russians preferring to give us hassle in the evening or at night, but this morning was different. It was so quiet it was eerie, funny peculiar. Our normal soundtrack – crumps, ack-ack, tank fire, mortars, small-arms fire in the distance – wasn't in service. Just as we were chatting about this or that, nothing of any note, I heard something quite new, something faint and muffled and distant. It grew louder but was hard to make out, the sound waves buffeting against the brick walls and heavy metal of the steelworks.

'Ssssh,' I told Misha. We listened hard.

Someone was making a speech on a loudspeaker system.

The dawn wind lifted, obscuring meaning, and then it died, and now we could make it out. It was the Russians, their message: 'Lay down your arms and surrender' on repeat.

'*Pizdiets!*' I whispered to Misha.

It was as if we were living inside the movie about the battle of Stalingrad in the Second World War, *Enemy at the Gates*. In one scene a Nazi propaganda lorry drives through the ruined city calling on the Soviet soldiers to surrender.

We listened some more with a kind of awe. Everything history and my experiences in Syria and Ukraine had taught me was that when an army started using this method to tell the other side to surrender it meant the climax was coming, that soon the battle for Mariupol and our steelworks would be lost and won. The Russians were so close they could try to browbeat us with their rubbish propaganda. Although I rejected the literal words, I knew – we all did – that the end was getting closer, that unless a miracle happened we would not be getting out of this twenty-first-century version of the siege of Stalingrad.

Our surreal guard duty over, Misha and I hurried downstairs to the bunker to see if there was any food left over from breakfast. No food: another grim omen. I helped deal with my hunger pains by tipping extra sugar into my coffee and then started walking towards the place we generally used as a makeshift latrine. But before I could make it, I was nabbed by the master sergeant, Mykola. He wanted me to help him load supplies for our infantry boys, who were fighting on the front line. We duly loaded up a shopping trolley, nicked from the superstore, with around thirty mortar bombs, and ran them over to a Zhiguli, a crappy Soviet copy of a 1970 Fiat 124.

That chore done, I returned to my mission, to answer the call of nature. I preferred to use a small maintenance room which was underground and, therefore, safe. Or safe-ish. The very last thing I wanted was to be bombed while emptying my bowels. Once I had finished doing my business, I was trudging up the stairs when one of the guys on duty shouted, '*Воздух!*' – '*Vosdukh!*', Russian for 'Air raid!' – our code signal for 'Take cover, there's a jet flying towards us!'

Down the stairs I clattered, before: 'WHOOSH!'

The bomb fell very close to where Sergeant Mykola and I had been a few minutes before I had taken my dump. Had I done my business first, and then helped him out with the mortars-on-shopping-trolley chore, we would have been toast.

David, my oppo from the mortar unit, called me over and told me the brigade was drawing up plans to break out of the steelworks and make a run for Ukrainian lines. To do that, the lads were using the plant's oxyacetylene welding equipment to boilerplate metal sheets on to our pick-ups to make them if not bulletproof, then bullet-resistant. We were turning the steelworks into a Mad Max production line. The electricity power supply long gone, the mechanics needed human muscle to lift the heavy metal sheets into place. A group of six big lads, including me, walked over to another part of the hangar to become human cranes. The mechanics' shop was an elephants' graveyard of dead killing machines: there, a BTR Soviet armoured personnel carrier, its tracks warped and twisted beyond use, here, a jeep with an engine block that now looked like 'The Brain of Morbius' – a *Doctor Who* episode. Lifting the plates to make our vehicles more secure was hard work and, for a time, watching the mechanics do their stuff, the sparks flying, lifted our spirits. We were doing something that might get us out of here. Soon, the mechanics' shop looked like the set of a dystopian science-fiction movie.

But the more I thought about it, the more I feared that the breakout was suicidal. Two cold facts were like spent ashes in my mouth. First, Mariupol had been encircled for nearly two months; second, the closest Ukrainian lines were 140 kilometres away. That's a hell of a drive in a war zone, even in a Mad Max vehicle. Still, the least I could do was document what the lads were up to. Also, at a deeper level, I sensed that the more I filmed our people alive, then if the Russians massacred us all, I was in some ways stacking up evidence of their future war crimes, and ideally for their war-crimes trials. So I hurried back to grab my camera to capture the sparks flying as yet another Mad Maxmobile was born.

The war around us ground on. At 3 p.m. we called it a day and returned to the bunker to be fed a plate of buckwheat: nothing special but better than nothing. My pal Shaun Pinner was in a fighting unit at the front line, beyond the steelworks' perimeter. I rarely got to see him and we were not allowed to use the radio to keep in touch. But I bumped into one of his comrades, on a visit to get provisions. I went over to him and asked how Shaun was, whether he was OK. Just a few days before I had powered up my phone to speak to Diana. The mobile phone-mast signal was pitifully weak but, if you were lucky, you could get through for a few minutes. She told me that Shaun's missus, Larysa, had been in touch and that she had got out

of Mariupol and was safe in Kirovograd, some 280 kilometres north of Mykolaiv. But how could I pass on that
message to my mate?

Aha! I ran into a ground-floor office space of the administration building, the top storeys of which had been
bombed, to find something to write with and on. On a
desk, someone had left some yellow sticky Post-it notes. I
grabbed one and with a pen wrote 'Everything is OK in
Ukraine, Russia has pulled out of Kyiv area and our guys
are doing good. Larysa is now in Kirovograd and safe.
However, we are fucked!'

I finished off my Post-it intimation of imminent death
with a smiley face, as you do. I rolled up the note, taped it,
and handed it to Shaun's comrade, asking him to play post-
man and deliver it to Shaun.

The lads had rigged an American Harris radio with a
long external antenna so that we could monitor HQ radio
traffic from one storey below ground, making us a little
safer but not as sweet as being in the bunker, which was
much deeper. While we did radio duty, our company commander and master sergeant were released to do other stuff
while I held the fort. The early evening shift from 4 p.m.
to 6 p.m. always tended to be when the Russians would
start getting lively. They had recently begun using their
tanks against us, fired from their positions about a klick or
two from the perimeter of the steelworks. Being bombed
was a constant threat and no shift would pass without
someone yelling 'Воздух!' – 'Vosdukh!' – and we all ducked
for cover as a Russian fighter jet screamed overhead. It got
on everyone's nerves, but mine were shot. To be fair, I was

perhaps the only one in the steelworks who had been bombed by both the Russians and the Americans. Of the two sides, I would say that it is better to be bombed – less bad, less accurate – by the Russians.

The jet gone past, I heard a tank fire in the distance: pop! You generally had three seconds, less, before the impact. I tripped downstairs, but thankfully, it missed. A call came through asking for someone to go across to the battalion HQ underneath the partially destroyed admin building – from where I had scribbled and looted my Post-it note for Shaun. Misha went on the errand while I manned the radio. Then a second pop, another tank shell coming our way. Once again, I fled downstairs, only to be challenged by our lieutenant, Ihor: 'What are you doing down here?'

For a second or two I thought I had dreamt the tank shell being fired and was a little embarrassed. So it was kind of a relief when there was an almighty crash up top, sending a shock wave and a ton of dust down the stairwell. My boss and I legged it into the bunker, sheltering behind its massive steel doors until we were confident that it was a one-off.

I went back up topside to see that the tank round had ricocheted off a massive water pipe, made of steel, and hit the plant directly above our bunker. We checked whether the radio was working and then it was back to the chores. Every time a tank shell, mortar round or bomb fell, I would call up our units to check if they were OK. On repeat.

Come ten o'clock there was a big commotion amongst the lads. After a bit the master sergeant, Mykola, explained that the decision had been made, the whole battalion was going to make a break for it through enemy lines. My oppo David was on the bunk next to me: 'Make sure your weapon is good to go,' I told him. 'Pack ammunition, dump useless shit, travel light.'

'We're going home, Johnny,' he replied.

'Yes,' I said.

I don't think either of us believed a word of it.

Some of the lads started spray-painting big Zs on our lorries so that we could pass off as Russian troops. Of course, it might be possible to bluff our way through one checkpoint. Two, maybe. Three at a push. But for a Ukrainian battalion to fake being Russian for 140 kilometres – the distance to our lines – struck me as being fucking crazy.

Around midnight I was called to do guard duty, replacing a guy who had been on stag for hours. Tons of our people arrived in the hangar, having been ordered to pull back from our outer lines, on foot and in BMP armoured cars, tanks and lorries. In all, we had around forty vehicles. The night was good, foggy with no moon, perfect for our mad mission. Time passed and nothing happened. People were still waiting around. The vehicles started driving off somewhere, but empty. When I was relieved from my guard duty, I returned to my bunk.

David, half-awake in his bunk, saw me and said with great tiredness in his voice, in English: 'Go to sleep, Johnny. No go home.'

I went back to my bed and lay down, wondering if we would ever get out of this hellhole. Later it turned out that, compared to where I was going to end up, the Illich steelworks was not a hellhole at all. It was, by comparison, a tropical island paradise.

Wake up. Duck. Make coffee. Duck. On repeat.

Same old, same old. In the morning I woke up, somehow angry that we hadn't used the perfect foggy weather to effect the breakout, but also knowing the idea was crazy-crazy. Around ten o'clock I broke the surface to go for my morning shit, the only luxury I had left in life. The maintenance room I regularly used had been locked, but there was a big room next door to it, which had become my new toilet area. As I walked towards the loo I saw a bunch of guys hanging outside the entrance to the tunnel leading to the battalion HQ.

That was odd. The boys told me high command had set up a Starlink connection and they were crowded around the battalion HQ entrance using the signal to piggyback on so that they could get phone service. I fired up my phone so that I could check in with my family. I sat down on a chair that was at the top of the stairs and leant against the railings, messaging Diana and my mum to let them know I was still OK. Even better I managed to get a call through to Diana. Her voice sounded surreally beautiful.

Call over, a great big orange ball of flame flashed in my right peripheral vision. First the orange, then the blast wave, smashing into my ears, eyes and down my lungs, then the smoke, thick and black. I staggered downstairs, into cover, reached the bottom, and bumped into David. We'd got so used to being hit – this time it was an artillery shell, I guess from a big gun, a howitzer, something like that – that it was bad form to overreact. David looked at me a little like Roger Moore in the Bond movies, raising that quizzical eyebrow, and the physical joke helped me get through the shock of the blast.

After a wary couple of minutes, we climbed up the stairs. The shell had fallen exactly where I'd planned to go to the toilet. Had I not stopped to look at my phone I might have been killed inside that room.

A second round came in, but using the precious phone signal was more important than staying alive. I'm exaggerating: we found that we could still piggyback on the signal from a point on a landing a level below the ground. Every five minutes another whizzbang would crash in above our heads while a whole gang of us hunched over our screens. It was like a scene from the movie *Oh! What a Lovely War* remade for the twenty-first century.

I decided to call my American friend Alex in Odessa. He was the first American I met when I arrived in Ukraine and was a good and loyal pal with great common sense. I trusted his judgement. He, too, had joined the Ukrainian Marines. To Diana and my mum I had been positive-ish; to Alex I told him the truth, that we had no hope, that we were fucked, and any day soon we would be captured. He briefed me, telling me what I should expect. I explained that I planned to destroy everything I had filmed on my camera if the time came, knowing that if the Russians understood I had been logging their war crimes I would be a target. As we were chatting, another shell burst one storey over my head.

'Did you hear that? We're getting smashed!' I said as the

dust rained down on my head. The shells were getting closer and more terrifying. We said our goodbyes and I continued checking the news on my phone. Another shell hit, closer than before, the dust and grit raining down on me. A sergeant told us to move further down the tunnel. Three more shells were fired, then, just like a sudden downpour, it all stopped.

I decided to leave the HQ tunnel, go upstairs, run across the open space, and get back down into the safety of our unit's bunker. I rocketed across the open ground like Forrest Gump and made it, my heart thumping in my chest.

My bunk was so deep below ground I felt safe. One of the other guys in our company had lent me his pipe, so I sat smoking a bit of tobacco I had begged from another and mulled through everything. How did the Russians find out that our senior commanders were based in the tunnel beneath the office block? Perhaps they got it out of one of our soldiers they had captured. How they would have done that did not bear thinking about. I couldn't see a good way out of the hole we were in. A breakout could have worked for a few klicks but not 140 kilometres: no way. So they either killed all of us, or we surrendered. If we surrendered, I knew that because of my social-media presence, I would be a target for them. What if they tortured me? Would I be able to handle it? Or would I give in?

Well, there was only one way to find out about that.

## Chapter Nine

# Hotel California

The Russians behaved correctly, more or less, but as soon as we were handed over to the Ukrainian quislings in the Donetsk People's Republic – the DPR – then the horrors started. After the soldier I nicknamed 'Sergeant Blue' realized from my passport that I was British and socked me in the face, then he really started to lay into me, jabs to my face and body, before a senior officer shouted at him to cut it out.

The beating stopped but Blue remained on a mission to give me a horrible time. He ripped off the yellow and blue Ukrainian flag patches velcroed to my uniform and placed them on top of my head, so I looked like some kind of dunce. Then he pushed me around, calling me a 'pede' – faggot in Russian – and ordered me to get down on my knees while at the same time he picked up his rifle. He was playing at mock executions, which is a fun game if you like that sort of thing. I didn't and still don't. For my own amusement, some of the time I pretended not to understand his Russian, but I certainly got the gist.

All the really bad stuff that happened to me was done by the quislings from the DPR, but the Russians were there too, controlling their puppets, taking down details, stepping out from the shadows now and then to log who had been captured and what they might know and not know. The Russians knew what was going on.

On Day Two of my arrest I was taken out of the warehouse. It was always scary when you were singled out, leaving the safety of the mass of fellow prisoners behind. On the other hand, any relief from the headbanging torture – having to rest your head against a wall for eleven hours, with your hands held behind your back or else – was a blessing. Outside the warehouse, I was taken to a Russian Tiger armoured car, one of the fanciest military vehicles they've got. It was not old Soviet rubbish but a machine made by a Russian-Chinese joint venture. In it were four officers. They never said so but I was pretty sure these Russian soldiers were, in fact, FSB – the new name for the KGB, the secret police. Although they were wearing Russian army uniform, they were in the Tiger and the rest of their kit was really top-notch: American-manufactured body armour, tablets, the kind of laptops not carried around by grunts. And their questions were smart: again, not your average Russian grunts.

A word about the FSB. Secret policemen have been a power in the land in Russia for centuries, but their clammy grip on Russia's soul strengthened with the October Revolution in 1917. The Bolshevik bloc of the Communist Party had fewer numbers than the Mensheviks, so in order to hold on to power, the knout, the cosh, and nine grams of lead in the back of the head stood in for the quaint ballot boxes and soapboxes we use in the West. After the Bolsheviks took power in October 1917, the secret police were first called the Cheka (short in Russian for 'All-Russian Extraordinary Commission'), whose leader Felix Dzerzhinsky ('Iron Felix') managed a regime of killing, torture and rule by fear. After ten years or so, by 1927, Stalin had emerged atop the Soviet bosses, whereupon he used the Cheka to silence his enemies, real or imagined. Towards the end of his life, Stalin remarked: 'I trust no one, not even myself.' The great book about the Soviet Union's relationship with the secret police is *Stalin and His Hangmen* by Donald Rayfield (2004). To begin with, the Communist Party was the more powerful institution, but as Stalin's paranoia engulfed the whole Soviet Union, the Cheka replaced it. Down the years, its name changed from Cheka to OGPU to NKVD to MVD to, after Stalin's death in 1953, the KGB. When the Soviet Union imploded in 1991, the KGB was broken up into three bits, but the key thing is that under Vladimir Putin the FSB are the people to fear.

The FSB officers knew exactly who I was. They took my military and veteran ID documents but they returned my passport. So the point I am making is that Russians can't blame ignorance on what was about to happen to me. They knew all about me.

That morning we were moved again to a second warehouse, where about 600 Ukrainian prisoners were being kept. I had not been fed or watered properly for twenty-four hours, more, and hunger was gnawing away at my insides. That's the thing about captivity, something I

hadn't figured out before it happened to me. Being a prisoner of war of an army that doesn't give a tuppenny damn
about the rules of war means that you are stripped of all,
or nearly all, the layers of civilization you are used to. The
freedom to eat or drink what you want to, to speak your
mind, to go for a walk or have a smoke or a drink of alcohol, to call your mum or your girlfriend, to take a piss or a
shit when you want to: all that was gone, taken from me.
The effect on me was far more powerful than I could ever
have imagined.

During the interrogation sessions it felt as though I was
standing naked in front of my captors. Not literally naked,
true, but in some spiritual sense that's what it was like. And
that eats away at your self-confidence. And then there's the
hunger.

To our just about suppressed joy, a Russian food truck
arrived and we got hot tea, buckwheat and a piece of bread.
It was no banquet but it was the first hot drink and proper
food I'd had for twenty-four hours – and remember we
were running out of food in our last two weeks at the
steelworks. Some new faces popped up, a mix of Russian
military and DPR agents, to take down our document
details all over again. This crew were far less fancy and on
it than the FSB. The redundancy of their bureaucracy was
a thing to marvel at, even though we were their prisoners.
The mood in the second warehouse seemed to be less sour
than the first. At least no one punched me on the nose.

After a bit, some agents from the DPR's MGB, the Ministry of State Security, rocked up. They singled me out of
the warehouse and took me to an empty side building

where a small group of prisoners were facing the wall to await yet more questioning. I was beginning to think that out of our battalion I was something of a catch. By the way, I worked out that they were the DPR's MGB because one of them was wearing a patch boasting exactly that. In simple terms, these people were the Donetsk oblast equivalent of the KGB/FSB.

And that was not good.

'You and Shaun Pinner are snipers.' That was the very first thing they said to me.

'No,' I replied and, in my rubbish Russian, went on to explain that we were not snipers but Ukrainian Marines.

'You are a mercenary.'

'No, I'm a marine. And I worked in a mortar unit.'

One of them ordered me to stand against a wall in the headbanger stress position while they found other guys in my unit to check out my story.

'If you are lying, you will pay for it.'

Two guys in my unit corroborated my story. I can't remember their names but I bless their little cotton socks. The MGB goons took me back to the main warehouse where I joined my mates a-headbanging.

The hours oozed by. I was no longer someone with agency but a pawn in someone else's chess game, and it was ever so very clear that I was on the losing side. After a long spell of muscle stress while I stood in that horrible unnatural position, head resting on the wall, hands behind my back, feet well away from the wall, the Donetsk MGB wanted to play with their new toy some more.

It was a different crew but they had the same DPR MGB

flashes as the previous lot. One of them was a short chubby fellow in his fifties. They handcuffed my hands in front of me and took me out to an SUV with Donetsk licence plates. I got that I was getting this special treatment because I was a foreigner. Once in the SUV, one of the men turned to me and said slowly in Russian: 'Now we're going to take you to be shot.'

I pretended that I had not understood what had just been said. We drove north-north-east – I could tell by the sun that it was around four o'clock in the afternoon – and I looked out of the SUV window at the cratered landscape, the burnt-down homes and the shattered churches.

So this was how I was going to die.

Five minutes. Ten. Fifteen. Half an hour. One whole hour. We didn't pull off the road but carried on. After a time, I dared to hope that the man who had told me I was going to be shot was just mucking around. We drove for roughly two hours and by this time I had figured out that you don't chauffeur a corpse-to-be around the countryside. Or, at least, not that often. I spent my time, bleakly, steadying myself for what I was damn sure was going to happen next: they were going to beat the living daylights out of me. I told myself not to react, not to fight back, not to do anything to make them angry. My sole focus was getting through the next twenty-four hours, to stay alive, to keep on breathing.

To exist.

At around 6 p.m., towards the end of our trip, they stuck a white plastic bag over my head to prevent me from working out where I was going to end up. But a plastic bag can of course suffocate you, so to keep me alive – and boy, that was good news – they punctured it with a precious few air holes. Through them I caught glimpses of the countryside slowly giving way to suburbs, then city streets. The SUV started to bounce up and down on cobbles. One of my mates in my battalion had told me that Donetsk is one of the few places in the Donbas where the roads are still paved that way. So, I calculated our direction and destination from the sun in the sky, roughly north-north-east, two hours travelling by car, the sound of cobble stones: we were in Donetsk.

I was Sherlock Holmes in a plastic bag.

The SUV pulled up. Welcome to UBOP. It sounds like an eighties roller disco, glitter-balls, fun, people dancing to 'Einstein a Go-Go', doing lines of coke in the loos and shagging in the car park. OK, that's the fantasy version. The real thing was UBOP, in Russian, Управление по Борьбе с Организованной Преступностью, and in English, Office for the Fight against Organized Crime of the Criminal Investigation Department.

And it's no fun. Full stop. It's a madhouse, a torture chamber and a boutique concentration camp, all rolled into one. For me, UBOP felt like the line in the Eagles song, 'Hotel California': I could check out any time I liked, but I could never leave.

They removed my handcuffs and took the plastic bag off my head. We had ended up in a sheltered car park, part of a rather grand building built in the tsar's time, complete with its own statue and exhibition hall, plus a big enclosed courtyard open to the sky. Leading off from the corridor were two rooms, about twelve by fifteen feet, smaller than the living room in our council house back home in Nottinghamshire. At the very worst point in my stay there were thirty-one 'guests' in that room. We slept together like sardines in a tin. But I am leaping ahead of myself.

One of my captors came up to me. They had taken off my plastic bag and I took a good look at him. Tall, thin, he had the same build as Rodney from *Only Fools and Horses*. I guessed he was in his late thirties, a flat black cowpat of dark hair on his head. He snapped something at me in Russian but his accent was so thick I didn't understand him. Politely, I asked him to repeat what he had just said. Rather than do this, he started to beat me with a thick truncheon. I knew if I hit back, that would be the end of me. He hit me hard on the head, the arms, and then brought savage force down on to my hand as I was raising it to protect my face. I fell to the floor and then he started kicking me in the head. I drifted in and out of consciousness. It was bad, really bad, far worse than I could ever have imagined.

He dragged me, semi-conscious, deeper into the UBOP building, and he carried on working on me. His line of interrogation was utterly banal. It would have been just plain stupid were it not for the storm of violence that was smashing into me.

'What's your rank?' The truncheon banged into my kidneys.

'How much were you paid?' Another kick to the head. And so on.

The catch was that, if I answered his question, he would hit me with the truncheon. If I didn't answer, he would hit me with the truncheon. The moronic questions, the sudden blows to the head with the truncheon, continued: question, thump, question, thump. It was formalized, our movements in lockstep, like we were dancing, locked in a sadomasochistic tango. I was his partner, a rose of blood clasped between my lips. There was something carnal, savage about our dance.

Suddenly, the tempo changed and the truncheon clobbered my head repeatedly. I raised my right fist to protect my skull and the truncheon crashed down. The pain was intense, utterly terrifying, beyond anything I had previously experienced in battle or the boxing ring. My hand ballooned in size and I feared bones had been broken. I cowered in a corner, mewing in pain.

His dark eyes followed me with a look of hate in them. Perhaps the hatred was only skin-deep. Deep down, he was a moron, perhaps the most stupid person it's ever been my misfortune to meet, or, at least, to be imprisoned by. The other constant, along with the shallow hate and the deep stupidity, was the stink of alcohol. My jailer hated me because he hated himself.

The beating stopped so he could take a break for a fag. Like many Ukrainians and Russians do, he dropped down to a crouching position, as if he was sitting on an invisible stool, better to enjoy his cigarette.

'Do you know who I am? I'm the man who's going to kill you. I'm the bringer of your death.'

There was no answer to that.

'Do you understand what I've done to you?'

I hadn't and I told him so. Still crouching, he flashed a

knife with a short blade and gestured to my left shoulder. It was only then that I got it, that along with the rain of blows with the truncheon, he had stabbed me. From then on, I called him Knifeman.

Bludgeoned by the blows to my head, in agony with my smashed-up hand, I was beginning to understand that he might well kill me.

'Do you want a quick death? Or a beautiful one?'

'A quick death,' I replied.

'I am going to make sure you have a beautiful death.' He was playing word games. By a beautiful death, he meant a slow, painful death, perhaps with lots of blood. Being stabbed scared me. I never anticipated being stabbed. Mentally, I was prepared for torture, for Knifeman to beat me black and blue, for suffering electric shocks, but not for being knifed.

The stabbing unmanned me. Back in the bunker in the steelworks, knowing, fearing that the game was up and we would have to surrender, I had tried to build a kind of wall in my mind, setting up the bricks to block the Russians from getting inside my head. They could hurt me, but they weren't going to control me. The stabbing knocked down my little brick wall, knocked it flat. From now on, I was going to do my level best to stay alive.

He left the cell. I lay on the floor as waves of pain beat through my body. I was not alone. My cell held two other prisoners, a man and a woman, both hooded. The guy was a stranger but, as for the woman, some strands of blood-orange hair were visible at the bottom of her hood. By the striking colour of her hair and her height – she was quite short, around five foot – I recognized Ruslana, a medic from my battalion. She was in her forties, very professional at her job and always up for a laugh.

Knifeman came back and sensed that I had clocked Ruslana. This being UBOP, he identified a new dancing partner. He handed his truncheon to Ruslana, ordering her to beat me. She refused so another of the guards hit me with it, all the harder. Knifeman then asked me to take my shirt off. The first thing he saw was my Ukrainian trident tattoo on my left arm. He beat me for that and then, uh-oh, he clocked the YPG tattoo I got when I fought with the Kurds in Syria.

'What's this?'

I told him I had been to Syria. The knife flashed in the dim light made by a bare electric bulb. He held it against my throat.

'Who were you with in Syria?'

Panicking, my mouth ran dry. I didn't know whether to speak or keep silent.

'If you don't tell me, I'm going to cut your ear off.'

I told him I was with the YPG, the Kurds, but he didn't understand who they were. Remember, my Russian was poor. It doesn't make for good-quality communication. There were two other guards with him and none of the three seemed to have the faintest idea of what had been happening in Syria apart from knowing that Russians were fighting there too. Finally, they worked out I had been to Kurdistan.

So they beat me some more.

Suddenly a fourth figure appeared and the beating

stopped, for a time. I had a friend, not in Jesus, but from the Russian intelligence service. He was a young blond officer, significantly smarter than Knifeman and the other goons. 'Blondie' held himself slightly apart from the beatings, as if they made him feel dirty or were inconvenient. Although I understood most of what was being said, every now and then Blondie translated phrases into English. He told me everything would stop if I told them the truth. I had only spoken the truth. Blondie then left the cell and the beating started anew, more savage than before.

When he returned, he said: 'Stop, you are going to kill him.'

About that, he was not wrong.

## CHAPTER TEN

# Mr Potato Head

Press play. The video comes to life: 'My name is Aiden Aslin . . . I thought in beginning Ukraine was good side. Eventually I see they don't make right decisions that would end war. They didn't want to negotiate with steps that could help end the war like peacefully. And then when President Putin signed new law to recognize Donbas and Luhansk as independent, Ukraine was given option to leave all of Donbas and Luhansk and Zelenskiy said no. And after this I see that Ukraine is not the good side because they started this war because they didn't want to leave.'

There are a number of strange things about this video. The first of which is that my speech is slurred. That's because of the concussion I had suffered the night before. The second is I have a six-inch gash and a great black bruise on my forehead where Knifeman hit me with his truncheon, my right eye is half-closed from the beating, and my face is cut. The third is that I'm talking pidgin English. As best I can, I'm trying to convey to people watching the video that I am only saying what I am saying – the

Kremlin's dark fairy tale that Ukraine started the war – because Knifeman, who had beaten seven shades of shit out of me the previous night, is standing directly behind the camera filming me talking rubbish.

Next to Knifeman was Andrey Rudenko, one of Russia's top propaganda merchants, who wanted to know why I had fought on the side of the Nazis in Ukraine. Rudenko is Squealer from George Orwell's *Animal Farm* in human form. He has been telling Kremlin lies about its war against Ukraine since 2014. He was in his thirties, quite good-looking, a smooth liar, and extremely aggressive towards me. All I knew was that I needed to play along otherwise this could get ugly for me. His translator was a skinny bleached-blonde woman, oozing a very Soviet chic from the time of late Brezhnev and wearing a strong perfume from the same era. I came to hate that smell. She could have been an Aeroflot hostess in 1979 before she hit the translate-for-torturers big time. Knifeman, Rudenko and Mrs Brezhnev must have thought they were the cats who got the cream, but, in hindsight, it was sour.

Two days previously I had posted my proof-of-life video from the steelworks just before we had surrendered. Then I had looked scared witless but my face was unhurt. And now I was talking Russian propaganda rubbish, and, entirely coincidentally, somehow had smashed my face in. How can I put this? My captors were fucking stupid. As horrific as it was for my mum – remember she collapsed at Funtopia back home when she saw how badly they had treated me – my wife Diana and the rest of the family to see me beaten up, the Russian agents who tortured me had provided to the world video proof of that torture. A lot of captives of the Russians and their proxies were tortured, horrifically so, far worse than me. But not that many could prove they were physically fine before being captured by the Russians, then tortured, and then had their wounds shown on camera. I suspect I might be the only one in that category. In a funny sort of way, my humiliating confession was an evidential boomerang, whirling back to the torturers to smash them in the face. Some time in the future I hope to catch up with Knifeman in The Hague. It would be good to meet him again, although this time he'll be the one who will be spending his nights in a cell.

The UBOP cell block was just one square room, smaller than the average council-house living room, about twelve feet by fifteen feet. There was no toilet, no window, no bunks or mattresses, just three benches and a few dirty blankets that stank to high heaven. Lice and cockroaches were our active cellmates. Light came from a naked electric bulb staring bleakly down on us, morning, noon and night. We had to piss in plastic water bottles; to shit, they let us out once a day in the morning for that, and a precious thirty minutes of walking around a courtyard. We got one small piece of bread: that was our only food for the entire day. It was just enough to keep us alive but nothing more. I would force myself to eat it as slowly as possible to try to curb my hunger and trick my brain into thinking I was tucking into a banquet. Worse than the gnawing hunger was our constant dehydration. The water ration was two two-litre bottles of water a day for the whole cell, though

the numbers varied from ten people to thirty-one. By the
way, a normal male should drink 3.7 litres of water a day –
so when the cell was full, this meant we were given less
than a twentieth of what we needed. This enforced thirst
was a torture all on its own, made all the worse by the lack
of ventilation. Human bodies generate a lot of heat. Pack
thirty people into a small room with no windows and
starve them of water, then their own bodies turn into a
kind of rack. We slept on the hard concrete floor, at times
so jammed together that we could only turn on our sides
when everybody else did. In the beginning I was scared to
trust my fellow prisoners. I feared that they might be spies.
This anxiety made that dark place all the more terrible.

And then there were the mind games. As I said, I served
with the Ukrainian Marines, never with the Azov Battalion, which is often criticized by the Russians and some
Western news sites for being far-right. The big picture here
is that, like every other country in the world, Ukraine has
some lunatics on the far-right, but they are on the periph-
ery, not the centre of the country's politics. Ukraine's
President Zelenskiy is Jewish, so is no friend of the far-right,
and at the last parliamentary elections the far-right failed to
get past the 5 per cent threshold for all political parties – so
they have no MPs. My take on the Azov Battalion is simple,
that Nazi is as Nazi does. The Azov people have never
invaded a peaceful democracy; Russia has. That said, I was
proud of being a Ukrainian Marine and no one had raised
any questions about my battalion. So, I didn't like it when
Knifeman ordered me to put on an Azov Battalion T-shirt.

Then they filmed me on a call to my brother, Nathan, wearing it. They were making me out to be, according to their perverse logic, a Nazi.

On my fifth day at UBOP, we had a new arrival. It was Major Yevhenii Bova, our battalion commander or, in Ukrainian military jargon, our KomBat. I remembered him in the steelworks just after the Russians had bombed our ammo dump, walking out in front of a great number of us, alone, then sitting down on a chair and smoking a cigarette. I was delighted to see him and whispered 'Zdorov'ya bazhayu' – 'Wishing you good health' – the polite greeting in the military to officers. He asked how I was. I told him about being beaten for hours and being stabbed, and that they were making me do propaganda. He rolled his eyes but there was no reproach. He understood how grim the Russians could be. I told him that just before I had surrendered I'd made a video letting people know we were about to be captured, and how stupid our jailers were in releasing a video of me with my face smashed in. I asked him how he had ended up at UBOP.

He told me they had lined up in a Mad Max convoy and shot out of Mariupol, but pretty quickly they were spotted and Russian artillery hit the BTR armoured car he was travelling in, knocking it out of action. Surrounded, outgunned and outmanned, they were forced to surrender. I told him that I had seen Victor, one of his majors, in the last few days and he was in good nick. It was cheering to see Bova because he was a great leader and a calm soul. He was the most senior officer in our horrible box at UBOP and he made sure that the food and water were shared equally and fairly between all of us. Every time I was taken out to do some more stupid propaganda and then brought back to the cell, I'd tell him what had happened and what they were making me do.

In the mornings when they would take us out into the courtyard for some fresh air, Bova would share his cigarettes with me and another marine from our brigade. The guards were wary of Bova and had let him keep his cigarettes. We would huddle round each other and smoke what we had until it was time to be put back in our cell. We tried to pass the time quietly, talking about the future or going over the mistakes of how the defence of Mariupol was handled.

After our surrender I had started to question my atheism. I've always thought people who do God a bit silly, but I won't lie. I had started looking for a higher power for comfort, maybe to trick myself into believing everything would be OK.

When he was beating me up, Knifeman had asked me if I was a Christian.

'Protestant,' I replied.

'You're not a Christian. You're scum,' he said. In a funny way, that made my new-found faith all the stronger. He didn't know it but I had made a makeshift cross out of what was left of my shoelaces and hid it from him.

Easter in UBOP was a surprise. In the evening the cell door opened and the guard gave us a bag containing *salo* – a Ukrainian type of bacon – a chocolate bar and other stuff. Given that we were being starved on a bit of bread a day, this was the best possible present. I still wrestled with my troubles with God or the absence thereof. Meanwhile, the mind games continued.

The darkest mind game of all was carried out by a fellow British subject – and someone born in Nottingham to boot. His defining characteristic was his spectacularly bald bonce. Let's call him Mr Potato Head. First of all, he assured his video audience that everything was above board, saying that filming prisoners of war was against the Geneva Convention, but that the rules of war didn't count here because I was a mercenary.

I was not.

He went on: 'But because we're all good, nice, polite people here, we shall adhere to the protocols and the covenants of the Geneva Convention . . . Aiden, would you like to confirm that you are speaking of your own will? There's not been any pressure or anything like that. You were fed, watered? You agree?'

'Yeah, I agree to this. I asked for this,' I replied.

'So, this is of your own will. There's not been any coercion? Your answers should be taken as your truthful representation of your actual position. There's going to be no coercion or anything like that.'

'Yeah.'

We were, of course, lying through our teeth.

Mr Potato Head's real name is Graham Phillips. There are rather too many useful idiots for the Kremlin, but only Phillips has taunted a Ukrainian prisoner of war, Volodymyr Zhemchuhov, who lost both hands and his eyes in a landmine blast. In 2016 Phillips put up a video on YouTube showing him climbing into a minivan marked with a red cross immediately before a prisoner exchange between several DPR pro-Kremlin separatists and Zhemchuhov. In his clunky Russian, Phillips mocks Zhemchuhov, who had stepped on a landmine in the Donbas in September 2015, then spent a year in separatist custody. Phillips said that Zhemchuhov spoke 'like a brainwashed zombie' and was 'not such a smart guy', accusing him of a sabotage plot that went wrong. There is no substance to this.

Zhemchuhov fired back, replying to the taunt about being not smart by saying that he was 'an educated man' familiar with what Phillips does, calling him a 'traitor, pro-Putin propaganda scum. Who made you come here to my Motherland? How much does Putin pay you? Go home'.

The Briton then said to the disabled Ukrainian prisoner: 'No one needs you any more because you lost your arms.'

Phillips' slavish support for the Kremlin has led to people calling him a traitor to Britain. He is that. Worse, he is a traitor to the human soul. When his bald head came into view in UBOP, my heart shivered. Physically and psychologically broken, I knew what was going to happen next. I was going to appear alongside Mr Potato Head in a Kremlin-sponsored YouTube video.

Before Phillips switched the camera on, he greeted Knifeman as a friend and told me that I was 'in good hands'. I was in fact in handcuffs, the scar on my forehead from Knifeman's truncheon still vivid, the bruising fading a little but still there, my right hand still swollen. Knifeman was one of two guards watching at the back. I suspected he still had his knife on him, the one with which he'd stabbed

me in the back. My stab wound was still weeping. It definitely needed stitches and I was worried about a serious
infection or sepsis. My captors had talked about giving me
medical treatment, but they never did. I had nothing with
which to clean the wound, so it stayed unwashed. Knifeman still had his truncheon with him.

Other than that, there was of course no coercion.

Phillips' first question floored me. It was about how the
stress generated by me had troubled my sister Shannon,
the mother of a very sick little boy. He had obviously read
an interview in a newspaper back home in England where
Shannon must have said that she was worried sick about
me. Phillips has no concept of below-the-belt. He went on
to say that my mother, too, was very worried about me.
He told me that I was lucky to be alive – I agreed with
him – then he moved on to Ukrainian atrocities. I can
honestly say that in my three years in the Ukrainian army
I didn't see a fellow soldier treat a Russian captive badly,
not once.

Phillips began: 'I dunno if you've seen the videos, I
know you've been quite active online, but can you describe
any of the videos you've seen of when Russian soldiers
have been taken, captured by Ukrainian soldiers and what's
happened to them?'

I am ashamed to say I went along with his rubbish propaganda. Forgive my cowardice but I felt I didn't have a
choice. I didn't want to be stabbed again. This was not
an academic question. Knifeman was standing a few feet
from me.

'From the videos that I've seen online of Russian soldiers being captured?' I replied. 'Ukrainian soldiers haven't adhered to the Geneva Conventions. There's been a lot of war crimes that have taken place from what I've seen. A lot of it's down to the Nazi groups.'

'See, let's get down to the nitty gritty. We're talking about absolute barbarism. We're talking about videos of Russian soldiers killed by stabbing them in the eyes. Tortured, mutilated, slaughtered by your colleagues. Your comments, Aiden? I mean, come on.'

Shrapnel from artillery can slice soldiers in all sorts of horrible ways, suggesting they may have been tortured when they haven't been. And explosions from mines often blind soldiers. Phillips should know because he had met Zhemchuhov.

He is not stupid, Graham Phillips. He read philosophy and history at the University of Dundee. But there is something very wrong about his judgement, as if he was missing something. Taunting a horribly injured soldier is an awful thing to do. I would worry about Phillips' immortal soul. Or the lack of it.

Phillips was born in Nottingham in 1979. After Dundee, he moved to London and became a British government propagandist, kind of, working for the now closed Central Office of Information, writing achingly banal press releases. He later moaned about how dull this work was. He first came to Ukraine in 2009 when he visited Dnipro for an England football game and fell in love with the place. He taught English and wrote a blog, 'Brit in Ukraine', a sleazy mix of stuff about prostitutes, sex tourists and soccer. Down the track, he deleted it. He had some talent, writing articles for the *New Statesman* and the *Kyiv Post*, but his 'great' story was about the death in 2008 of Barry Pring, aged forty-seven, a wealthy British IT consultant.

Pring, originally from Devon, had moved to Ukraine to marry a primary-school teacher and dancer called Julianna Ziuzina in a whirlwind romance. On their first wedding anniversary the couple had just been celebrating in a restaurant in Kyiv. When they could not track down a taxi, they climbed over a guard rail and on to the hard shoulder of a dual carriageway, before Julianna returned to the restaurant to collect a glove she had left under the table. Pring was then killed on the unlit road by a hit-and-run driver in a car with false number plates. Pring's family suspected Ziuzina, now known as Moore, of ordering a hit. In 2013, Phillips self-published his book on the story, *Ukraine – Men, Women, Sex, Murder.* A first inquest in Devon in January 2017 concluded that Pring had been unlawfully killed, but this was later quashed by the high court. A second inquest followed in Bristol. The papers reported that Judge Paul Matthews, sitting as a senior coroner, ruled that there had been no conspiracy to kill: 'There is not a single piece of direct evidence to show that there was any such conspiracy, or that if there was, who was involved. Instead, the Pring family put forward a number of allegations based on circumstantial evidence which they say, when taken together, collectively suggest that Julianna Moore was criminally involved in organizing the death of her husband, Barry Pring, and was indeed guilty of his murder.'

Pring had owned three properties in the London area and a flat in Kyiv, but the judge described him as 'not that wealthy' as these were mortgaged, which Moore knew. She had told the inquest that her life would have been 'much more comfortable financially' if Pring was alive and denied any involvement in his death.

The judge said: 'If this was a murder, it was a curious, risky and inept way to carry it out.' He added: 'I am not persuaded that there ever was a conspiracy to murder Barry Pring, much less that Julianna Moore was part of it.'

The innocent widow started legal action against Phillips, and his sorry nonsense of a book was withdrawn from sale, pulped.

In 2013, Putin's puppet in the Ukrainian presidency, Viktor Yanukovych, backtracked on getting closer to the European Union and switched over to the Russians. Ukraine rebelled and the Maidan Revolution broke out in 2014. From the word go, Phillips sided with the Kremlin's line. His doggish devotion to the killer in the Kremlin was picked up by RT, Russia's patsy TV channel, and he was interviewed. When Russia staged its first war on Ukraine in the spring of that year, Phillips turned full Lord Haw-Haw, siding with the invaders, not the invaded.

He started 'reporting' – if reporting it was – freelance, for RT, after the station's crews were banned from Ukraine. He managed to get captured by the Ukrainians, who detained him for a day, then released him, on condition that he leave the country for good. He flew out, went back to Russia, then crossed over into Russian-occupied Ukraine. RT used him for a bit but never gave him a job.

That may be because he was more useful to Russia's dark state, playing the role of 'independent journalist'; it may also be because he was so unpleasant as to be unemployable. I suspect the latter.

When Malaysia Airlines MH17 was blown out of the sky by a Russian BUK missile in July 2014, killing all 298 people on board, Phillips sided with the mass murderers. Two years later, he went to the Berlin offices of Correctiv, seeking an interview with the journalist Marcus Bensmann, who was investigating the tragedy. Things turned nasty and Phillips refused to leave, filming himself shouting 'Lying press!' That phrase was first made popular in German, *Lügenpresse*, by Adolf Hitler.

You get the drift.

When Phillips taunted me about Russian soldiers being mutilated by Ukrainian soldiers, I replied: 'If I ever saw anyone doing anything like that, I'll try to intervene because first and foremost, just because it's the enemy, they shouldn't be treated any less once they drop their rifle. And I think the people that do these crimes, they should be punished to the fullest extent, which with the Ukrainian military, I doubt they're going to even care about it.'

Phillips was on a roll, his body swaggering as he hammered out his words: 'We're talking about Ukrainian soldiers. I'm going to use a few choice words to describe them. Animals? Yeah. Scumbags. Barbarians. Your comrades. Aiden, how has this ended up that you are on that side?'

'I made stupid choice.'

As with the first rubbish propaganda interview, I was

deliberately speaking bad English. You should say: 'I made a stupid choice.' By talking stupid English, I was trying to convey that this interview was taking place under coercion. The stupid English trick was OK with the guy in the black leather jacket because he didn't speak English at all, and the Soviet-era translator's facility with the language of Shakespeare wasn't that great, but I was pulling the same trick with Phillips. He was too up himself to notice. Before I was captured I had told my family that I would alert them to the fact that I was talking under duress by scratching my nose. You would have suspected I had a massive coke habit by the frequency with which I pawed my schnozzer during that interview. Again, Phillips was too much of a narcissist to notice.

By the way, Phillips did give me some lines to repeat, but most of the time I freewheeled it, knowing full well what the key Russian propaganda lines were. 'I easily misread the information and joined the wrong side,' I continued.

Phillips then recalls the very funny sketch by two British comedians, David Mitchell and Robert Webb, both dressed up in hideous black SS uniforms. Mitchell says to Webb: 'Are we the baddies?'

Phillips asked me if I had seen the sketch and I said, yes, and then repeated the catchphrase: 'Are we the bad guys?'

Back in the day, Phillips had a go at stand-up comedy, alongside Frankie Boyle and Miles Jupp. Comedy's loss was the Kremlin's gain. I said it was only when we were in Mariupol that I'd started to realize the truth about Ukraine. Phillips probed me about how come I ended up here. My answer was to flatter him, to say that originally I was pro-Russian, that I had followed his work, but that I'd met a friend in Syria who told me that Ukraine was in the right. I played thick: 'I was easily misled.' He took the bait, calling me 'impressionable'.

Once again, he returned the conversation to his favourite topic: 'You've been serving for years in the Ukrainian army. Obviously, you are socially aware in terms of social media and all the rest of it. In that time, you must have surely done some research, looked at Google. You must have seen the signs that Azov wear the Wolfsangel?'

Indeed, the Azov Battalion do. The Wolfsangel – meaning 'wolf hook' or better translated as 'wolf trap' – is an ancient German symbol based on a Z-shaped iron trap. It was used during the Thirty Years War and popped up again and again as a symbol of ferocious force, adopted by the Nazi Party and sundry German Wehrmacht and SS units, for example, the massacre-committing Waffen-SS Division Das Reich. The fly in Phillips' ointment is that the Russians at the start of the war painted a great big Z on their tanks prior to their big invasion. Once again, Nazi is as Nazi does. But I did not dare say what I actually thought.

'You must have worked out that these guys are Nazis?'

I said I only properly understood that after we retreated back into Mariupol and we rubbed shoulders with the Azov Battalion. He then played the fellow Brit card: 'I'm going to give you the opportunity then from a Brit to a Brit. In your own words, your relationship now. What should people in the UK know and how should they relate to the Azov Battalion?'

I waffled on about their leader, not very coherently.

'They wear Nazi symbols, they have Nazi salutes,' said
Phillips.

'The Wolfsangel, they wear that proudly,' I said, following his line. 'A lot of the traditions they have are from
Nazi military traditions that they try to re-enact.'

'So surely,' said Phillips, 'at some point you've got to
where you are, where you're in captivity, but you are lucky
to be alive. There can be people watching this from all over
the UK. OK. So you've got to where you are, but surely
there were so many steps along the way that you could
have, of your own will, said, "Look, I'm not being part
of this. I'm not fighting with what are" – and I'm not putting words in your mouth, I'm simply stating objective
facts – "I'm not fighting with Nazis."'

He was putting words into my mouth. The Azov
Battalion were defending their country from a fascist
regime that invaded a democracy and tortured its soldiers.
I should know.

'Yeah,' I said. 'I just never came into contact with them
until the Mariupol situation came into play. I was hoping
to finish my contract and go home, leave Ukraine with my
wife. But this war happened because Ukraine can't, doesn't
want peace,' I lied.

Then he moved on to what I had been up to.

'So, the past six months you'd be preparing artillery,
which has then been fired. And where has that been fired?'

I told him that we had been firing at enemy positions.

'And you say "enemy positions". But we are now in the
city [Donetsk] where for the last eight years, Ukrainian
forces have been shelling, not enemy positions, but civilians,

killing thousands of civilians, children, for eight years. So, you're telling me that you think that you were shelling military positions and yet for eight years your colleagues have been openly and in fact glorifying and celebrating and shelling, killing and inflicting untold misery and suffering on the people of Donetsk.'

The correct answer would have been: 'Listen, you stupid creep, the maximum range of a 120mm heavy mortar is eight miles. Donetsk is seventy miles from where we were based before we moved even further back to Mariupol. So our unit could not possibly have hit Donetsk. The truth is that Russian fire was far, far more intense. For whole chunks of time, we were forbidden from firing back because we were honouring a ceasefire you fuckers kept on breaking. And the big picture, Mr Potato Head, is that Russia invaded a peaceful Ukraine. Innocents die in all wars. But Russia started it.'

Instead of saying that, what I actually thought, I said 'Yeah', effectively agreeing with his rubbish. Then I played up my anxieties about Diana, turning that I had wanted to make sure she was safe into a desire to desert, but that proved to be impossible. The duel continued.

'I didn't want this war,' I told him. Then I blathered on for a bit about my contract woes, that when I had signed up for another year I had expected that year would be spent training in Mykolaiv, not being deployed again on the front line. That much was true. My words were pretty clumsy, but then so were his. My excuse was that I was being starved and dehydrated and had been beaten unconscious and stabbed a few days before. He had no excuses.

'I just can't quite believe that, if I'm being honest,' said Phillips.

This interview was psychological torture. I still have trouble, flashbacks, dealing with this, how Graham Phillips took apart my integrity, long after my physical wounds have healed. I've read that victims of psychological torture suffer far more than those who experience physical abuse. That chimes with my own experience. I still have nightmares about these hours.

Every time he pushed me, I tried to feed the mad dog a biscuit. I'd watched enough of the Kremlin's rubbish to know their main propaganda lines, so I echoed them: 'There was, always, every opportunity for Ukraine to de-escalate. They blatantly ignored every one.'

The whole world knows that Russia's bite out of Ukraine's apple is a death knell to the post-Second World War peace settlement, that nation states must have compelling reasons to invade other nations, and that Russia's logic for war, that Ukraine is a Nazi state though its president is Jewish, is absurd. But Graham Phillips doesn't. He is a believer in the legitimacy of the Donetsk and Luhansk People's Republics along with Syria and North Korea. It's a joke – but not a funny one.

'Ukraine had eight years to recognize the republic, to recognize the results of the referendum in 2014,' he said.

The referendum was a bleak puppet show, only held after hundreds of thousands of loyal Ukrainians had fled to other parts of the country for safety.

'My biggest problem with the Ukrainian authorities,' I lied, 'was the non-recognition of Crimea as Russian territory. Because, as you said, it's been eight years regardless of what anyone thinks.'

'Tell me, whose territory is Crimea? Russian? And Donetsk and Luhansk People's Republics?'

'Independent.'

He returned to his G spot, the Nazis of the Azov Battalion. What did I make of them?

'Fanatics, criminals, Nazis.'

'OK. You accept that. You're lucky.'

'Yeah, I'm lucky. And I'm grateful.'

Everything was tickety-boo between us.

'How's your detention? Can you describe your circumstances, your situation?'

'It's been good. It's better than what I was expecting it to be.'

Once again, my stab wound was still weeping, my head and body still ached from the beating, I had a smashed-up face and a gash on my forehead.

'Aiden, as we've discussed, your family are worried about you. You'd like to have the opportunity to say some words to camera to speak directly to camera, to your family.'

This was payback for my grovelling and I took the opportunity, big time: 'So Diana, Diana my wife, I want you to know I love you . . . My mother, my brother, and the rest of my family. I also love you and I hope to see you guys soon.'

'You understand,' Phillips said smoothly, 'we're out of the jurisdiction here of the British government. As it's being positioned in the British media, you're being held by bad Russians. Your own Twitter account is pumping out a stream of anti-Russian bile and hatred. As you're being positioned in Sky, the BBC, the *Daily Mail*, et cetera, as some kind of hero who went to fight for Ukraine. But now you've ended up being taken by the Russians, who you told the worst things about. And yet here you are in captivity for a week. You look absolutely OK to me. Yeah, in decent health.'

Earlier I used the phrase 'mind game'. What I had meant to write was 'mind fuck'.

'Firstly,' I replied, 'for people who say I am a hero, I'm not a hero. I tried to desert and it's not something a hero would do. Secondly, my treatment's been good. I've not been beaten or anything.'

Liar, Aslin, liar. 'It's been better than what I actually thought it was going to be like,' I continued. 'When we were surrendering, I was scared, scared to death of what might happen. I thought I was going to be lined up and shot. But it's been quite the opposite. We've been given food, water, access to speaking to journalists.'

Well, kind of. The day before Phillips turned up, an Italian journalist, Manuele Bonaccorsi, had interviewed me. This time there were no goons in the room: Bonaccorsi had made that a condition of the interview. He went out of his way to insist on that, so I could 'speak freely'. But, of course, I dared not. I knew that if I told him the truth, that I had been beaten, stabbed and knocked unconscious, then the moment the Italian's report went online I would be in real danger. When he asked me about how I was being treated, I told him the same lies I told Phillips.

But Bonaccorsi did not pick at my psychological wounds in the same revolting way that Phillips did.

Was I a mercenary? he had asked. Yes, I told him. Which company did I work for as a mercenary? I had a contract with the Ukrainian Ministry of Defence, I said. For this book, Bonaccorsi explained that he understood from my conflicting answers that I had been compelled by my captors to say that I was a mercenary, but he realized from my answer to his follow-up question that I was not – and he reported that.

At the end of the interview, he gave me some hand-rolled cigarettes with Italian tobacco, which he told me to hide when I got back to my cell. The contrast with Phillips was like that between day and night.

Back to Phillips, who banked my gratitude and then went back on to the attack: 'I'd like to get your thoughts on the fact that your colleagues committed barbarism and brutality towards Russian prisoners of war. Well, an interesting point is, let's, let's be honest here. Let's say things as they are. You have appealed for Russia to adhere to the Geneva Convention. Technically, you're a mercenary, so that doesn't apply to you.'

But, technically, legally or in any other way, I wasn't a mercenary. I was a serving soldier with a contract with the Ukrainian Ministry of Defence and had residency because of that. A mercenary works for a private company, not a state. Nor was it for Phillips to define the law. I flexed my wrists in my handcuffs and put up with more of the same.

'However, you're still being treated well,' Phillips continued smoothly, Knifeman just behind him. 'You're here, we are speaking, you're fed, you're watered, et cetera. Well, on the other side, we've seen Russian servicemen butchered, tortured, slaughtered by your colleagues, your comrades. I mean, how does that make you feel?'

'It annoys me because I did believe in Ukraine. But as I said, the real reality of what's behind a lot of the people who seem nice, the reality of the actions has been shown, and they're not as good as they say they are. Especially with the videos that we've all seen. We're . . .'

'Talking about evil,' he interrupted.

'Yes. This is stuff that is comparable to what the Nazis did when they would capture prisoners.'

He did a quick drive-by shooting of Stepan Bandera – I agreed with him, obviously – and then it was back to how the two sides were seen: 'Let's break it down. Aiden, in the United Kingdom, in the British media, it's categorically delineated down the lines of the Ukrainians are the good guys, the Russians are the bad guys. Tell me from one who knows, with experience of both sides, what's the reality?'

'Ukraine's not the good guys.'

He pushed me to say that fellow Brits tempted to fight alongside the Ukrainians would be foolish to do so. Oh yes, I said: 'Don't do it. You'll be used. Obviously to the person that will be viewing this, who is thinking about going, you'll be thinking, "It's someone putting this into my mouth." But I tell you now one hundred per cent, if you go, you are an idiot. Like myself, we were used, easily tossed aside when forgotten about. If there's people that think they're going to be coming out to be the hero, don't even think about coming out. No point. And the British

government need to stop . . . stop . . . I can't think of the
word . . .'

'Supporting.'

'Stop supporting citizens to go fight alongside the
Ukrainians.'

Then he turned up the heat, bringing up 'the penalty in
the Donetsk People's Republic for being a mercenary . . .
Do you accept that you're a mercenary?'

'I'm a mercenary. Ah-huh.'

'It's the death penalty. Can you give a reason as to why
that shouldn't apply to you?'

Mercy – that's what my answer boiled down to. He
asked me to address the Russian people who, he said, were
very angry with me.

'So, I know you hate me and *sorry* can only get you so
many emotions, but it doesn't express my true apologies
for being in the circumstances in which I am. If I could
take it back, I would've left long ago. But that's not the
case. What's done is done. All I can ask is that you forgive
me and accept that I surrendered and tried to desert from
the Ukrainian forces. I can't think of much more.'

I was utterly exhausted, so emptied out by stress that I
could not even be bothered to defend myself. On it went.

'From a concrete point of view,' he asked, 'what would
you be willing to do to atone for the evil that you admit
you've been a part of? How can you propose that you
would make amends for that?'

Atone for the evil? 'I would help rebuild, there's people
that have no homes, they've lost their families.'

'What is Ukraine for you now? What does it represent?'

'Disloyalty . . . forgetful. I can't remember these words. It's been so long since I used English.'

He goaded me some more. My answers were getting more and more feeble. I was sick of this nonsense, sick of him, sick of my cowardice. But Knifeman was still there, lurking. I was still a prisoner, held against my will and in fear for my life.

'You've got a tattoo that says "Happy days". What would you like to say to Boris Johnson in terms of his unconditional support of Ukraine, what would you like to say to him?'

'So, Boris Johnson, if you're watching this video, obviously you are aware of my situation and this situation in this area. Firstly, I'd like to say, help end this war. And I don't mean militarily, I mean help it be achieved by peace. Eight years is a long time for war. And with the new edition of this operation, we need to help finish it so civilians can return to their lives without threat.'

'And how should it be finished? On what terms?'

'Donetsk, Luhansk and Crimea recognized as Russian territory. That's a reasonable request. I can't see why they wouldn't accept that.' Those three oblasts are, of course, part of Ukraine.

Phillips was wholly on message with my torturers. Towards the end of the interview, he switched off the camera and suggested that I make a direct appeal to Boris Johnson, the then British prime minister. He switched back on, and off I went: 'So, Boris Johnson, I need you to listen. The DPR authorities have given the chance for us to be exchanged and all they ask is that we are exchanged for Viktor Medvedchuk.'

They wanted a trade. Medvedchuk was a Ukrainian traitor. The question was, would the Ukrainians do the trade before the Russians had their proxies execute me for murder?

Phillips' last trick was the most revolting.

'Now I'm going to get a load of hassle, a load of stick from people saying that the terrible, the evil, criminal propagandist Graham Phillips interrogated poor Aiden Aslin, et cetera, et cetera. From your side, we've chatted today, one man to another. How's it been for you?'

I talked straight down the barrel of the camera lens: 'It's been good. I just want to point out he didn't get called to me. I asked, I knew about Graham, I asked to speak to him because Graham is British. Don't just jump on the bandwagon. Look into the interview that we're doing now. It's legit.'

No, it wasn't. For Phillips to coerce false propaganda from a prisoner of war on pain of torture is not good. As with Knifeman, I hope to meet Phillips again at The Hague, with me in the witness box and him in the dock. The Geneva Convention is out of date and does not directly address whether filming a prisoner of war is unlawful or not. But Article 13, paragraph 2 of the Third Geneva Convention of 1949 states that:

'. . . prisoners of war must at all times be protected, particularly against acts of violence or intimidation and against insults and public curiosity.'

That phrase 'public curiosity' is elderly, but sticking a camera in the face of a blind double amputee breaches that. Phillips, for my money, insulted and sought to intimidate Ukrainian POW Volodymyr Zhemchuhov. Phillips exposed me to 'public curiosity' too, no doubt about that. The fresh scar on my forehead was powerful evidence that I had been the victim of violence. Phillips didn't hit me, but he was very pally with Knifeman who had. Take his conduct with Zhemchuhov and me together, I suggest that demonstrates a pattern of Phillips violating Article 13, paragraph 2, as big as a barn door.

Once the camera had been switched off, Phillips translated into Russian the key points of everything I had said to Knifeman.

Later on, Graham Phillips defended his interview with me, saying he had 'nothing to hide', arguing that I had 'requested the interview . . . Let anyone serious present any real charges against me, and I'll fully answer all of them – I'm an independent journalist of complete integrity and absolutely sound of conscience and ethics.'

I disagree. To me, Graham Phillips is evil.

## Chapter Eleven

# 'What is your 11-digit V5C reference number, please?'

I am a prisoner of war in an alternative universe. In this dystopian place I am accused, falsely, of being a mercenary. If I insist I am not one, then I fear I'll get stabbed again by Knifeman. Yet being considered a mercenary means I am not a prisoner of war but a war criminal. And being a mercenary carries the death sentence. So, I can end up dead if I deny being one. But if I accept their false framing of me as a mercenary, then I can also end up dead. My strategy is to choose putting off being stabbed again in the immediate future over certain death in the medium-term future. By comparison, *Catch-22* was a walk in the park.

I had not been tried yet. My first experience of the DPR judicial system was poor. And then it got worse, a lot worse, very quickly.

In the early morning I was taken out of my cell, cuffed, and led to another room in Hotel California. I was still stiff from my beating, the scar still vivid on my forehead, my black eye still bleeding obvious. My new inquisitor carried himself like some kind of cop, but he was working for a fake state controlled by a fascist dictator next door, so I didn't expect much attention to the niceties of the rule of law. My low expectations were too high.

The wannabe cop was no Jack Regan from *The Sweeney*. More child than man, so fresh-faced that he looked to be prepubescent, slim, frail, he spent the whole time playing such a hard man it struck me that he was, like everyone else in the Mickey Mouse state of the DPR, hideously insecure. He pulled out a naff hi-vis jacket and gestured for me to look at the back of it, on which was written 'Russian Investigative Committee' – kind of localese for FBI, but I wasn't falling for the con. This guy wasn't Billy Big Balls from Moscow but a local hick, mucking about.

He sat down behind a desk with a laptop and a camera set up behind him and said: 'Let's start.' I gave the boy my life story, more or less. I left out the bit about me almost dying because of the wood-burning stove. My version of fighting correctly, according to the rules of war, did not please him. He stopped me and made the wanking gesture, meaning: 'Tell me what I want to hear or I will fuck you!'

He asked me the same kind of questions as Knifeman had done: 'Are you working for the CIA? Are you working for British intelligence?' I told him no to both.

'Are you in the SAS?'

'Look at me, I'm fat,' I replied, hoping that would be the end of that. It wasn't.

'Have you had any contact with them?'

'No,' I said, which was true but not quite the whole

truth. Through a friend of a friend, I had been contacted by someone in the British army intelligence corps. They phoned me up from time to time and I told them exactly what I would tell anyone down the pub if I had been at home, that Ukrainian army morale was good, the training was good, but we needed far more and far better anti-aircraft defence. To be honest, I told them nothing more than I told Sky News, nothing that would have compromised Ukrainian operational security.

After two hours of this nonsense, the kid cop packed it in and I was returned to the cell where the others asked me if I had been beaten. No, I told them. Not long after, my name was called again and I walked to the door of the cell, waited to be cuffed, then I shuffled along behind my guards with my head bowed low. These short walks out of the cell shredded my nerves. You never knew what was going to happen to you.

This time I was going to have a long natter with Mikhail Popov, the press officer of the DPR MGB. I had never met a secret-police press officer before and won't mind if I never ever do again. Popov was young, handsome, cocksure and extremely stupid. Quite how devoid of human intelligence he was is something to marvel at, like an extraordinary rock formation or a glass of good Italian red wine or a meteor lighting up the night sky. I have met a lot of stupid people in my life, but Popov takes the biscuit factory.

Popov and his pal 'Vlad' – a thickset secret-police type, hence my nickname for him – were running the DPR's campaign to get Ukraine to agree to trade me and my fellow Brit, Shaun Pinner, for their number-one traitor,

Viktor Medvedchuk. Perhaps the best way to explain what kind of man we are dealing with is not to describe him as a 'Ukrainian oligarch' or 'pro-Kremlin patsy politician', but just to name his youngest daughter's godfather: one Vladimir Putin.

The word on the streets of Kyiv about Medvedchuk is that his old man collaborated with the Nazis and that Viktor did the same with the Soviet KGB. When he was a student in Kyiv in the 1970s, the story goes, he was co-opted to work as a police officer. One day he and another policeman caught a youth behaving in an anti-social way. However, the youth had connections, his father was a high-up, and things looked bad for Medvedchuk until the KGB made him an offer he couldn't refuse. 'Work with us' – spy for us, that meant – 'or you are out of university.' Medvedchuk complied and the Soviet secret state had him. As a young defence lawyer he got three gigs playing defence lawyer for three Ukrainian dissident poets. The catch was that his clients hated him, suspecting he was actually batting for the other side. First, in 1979, Medvedchuk defended the dissident poet Yuriy Lytvyn, who told the court: 'The passivity of my defence lawyer Medvedchuk is not due to professional incompetence but to the orders he got from above: he does not dare tell how the system operated against me.' Lytvyn died in a prison hospital in Perm Oblast in September 1984. One year later another dissident poet, Vasyl Stus, was tried for 'anti-Soviet activities'. Stus had just got out of prison but was in trouble again because he helped organize Ukraine's Charter 77 group, as virtually everybody else, including Lytvyn, had been locked up or died in mysterious circumstances. Stus wrote: 'Psychologically, I understood that the prison gates had already opened for me and that any day now they would close behind me – and close for a long time. But what was I supposed to do? Ukrainians were not able to leave the country, and anyway I didn't particularly want to go beyond our borders since who then, here, in Great Ukraine, would become the voice of indignation and protest? This was my fate, and you don't choose your fate. You accept it, whatever that fate may be.'

His fate was to be defended by Medvedchuk. Stus rejected this court-appointed lawyer because, according to his widow, 'he immediately felt that Medvedchuk was an aggressive Komsomol' – the Soviet Youth organization, a bit like the Hitler Youth – 'type person, he didn't protect him, he didn't want to understand him, and, in fact, he was not interested in his defence.' But justice in the Soviet Union was a black farce and Stus was stuck with Medvedchuk, who made a speech calling for his client to be found guilty. Which he duly was. Sent to the gulag in the Russian city of Perm, Stus went on hunger strike and died behind bars in September 1985.

The third dissident poet who had the misfortune to be defended by Medvedchuk was Mikola Kuntsevich. His lawyer was accused of pouring 'more dirt on him than the prosecution'. After Medvedchuk asked the court to dismiss one of Kuntsevich's motions, the poet challenged him and repeated the challenge several times, but each time the court dismissed it. Medvedchuk told the court: 'I completely agree with the comrade prosecutor in determining the sentence. But, for reasons incomprehensible to me, the comrade prosecutor forgot that the defendant had not yet finished one year and nine months from the previous sentence. I consider it necessary to add this period to the new sentence.' The court agreed with the anti-defence defence lawyer and the poet got a longer sentence. Kuntsevich survived the gulag but died in 2021.

So while Vladimir Putin was a hard-working secret policeman, Medvedchuk was doing his bit to subvert the rule of law in Soviet Ukraine by being more horrible to dissidents charged with rubbish offences than the prosecution. Come Ukraine's independence, he still steered to the Russian side of the street. For three years in the early noughties, he was head of pro-Russian Leonid Kuchma's presidential administration. While doing so, he was so close to the Kremlin that, as already noted, Putin became the godfather to his youngest daughter. People say that politics in Ukraine is corrupt. Well, maybe. It is true to say that by the turn of the decade Medvedchuk was worth close to $500 million and had his own super-yacht and private plane. After the Russian invasion of Crimea, Donetsk and Luhansk, Putin shuffled his pack of Ukrainian proxies and Medvedchuk's name popped up again and again as one of two contenders to be Russia's favourite as Ukraine's next leader. However, in May 2021 Ukraine busted him for a series of offences and he was placed under house arrest. Just a few days after the big war started in February 2022, Medvedchuk fled house arrest and vanished. In truth, he was holed up in a fancy three-storey house in Kyiv until Ukrainian intelligence, the SBU, busted him on

12 April – the very same day I had surrendered. Photos of him in Ukrainian army uniform and handcuffed, looking depressed but not beaten up, appeared not long after mine.

The Russians moved fast to get their man back. It became a constant of my life in captivity. I would be wheeled into the propaganda room in UBOP, seated on a chair, and invited to say my piece to a phone on speaker while being filmed. I got to know my patter by heart: 'Hello, my name is Aiden Aslin and I am a British prisoner of war being held in eastern Ukraine's Donetsk region, and the authorities here want to exchange me and fellow British detainee Shaun Pinner for Viktor Medvedchuk.'

The tricky problem for the British government is that only North Korea and Syria had recognized the DPR, therefore engaging with the authorities in Donetsk was something that Whitehall didn't want to do at all. I was stuck in limbo. That didn't mean I could opt out of this process. The calls that got through were many and various, and I've forgotten a lot of them. The ones that stand out start with getting through to the switchboard of Number 10 to try to talk to the then prime minister, Boris Johnson. He didn't come on the line, however I did speak to a duty clerk who noted everything I told him but was extremely non-committal. They put me through to the Foreign Office, where I got the same treatment as from Number 10, and to the House of Commons so I could talk to my Newark MP, Robert Jenrick, or his office. Jenrick stood up for me, calling out Graham Phillips as having committed a potential war crime by forcing me to take part in his black propaganda, though later I read that

Jenrick, before he became a Tory MP, had spent time making money in Moscow. The *Sun* newspaper was as good as gold: they took every call I made but, understanding that I was under duress, they never ran a word of my quotes. I am embarrassed to say that when my captors called the *Guardian*, its switchboard couldn't find a reporter to talk to me, so that was a dud.

When they were in a good mood and felt that I had got some traction with the Foreign Office, my captors would call my mum. These calls were always incredibly stressful for her and me, because the whole point of what UBOP, Knifeman, Graham Phillips, Popov and Vlad were doing was to push me into panicking so much that the British government would pile on the pressure with the Ukrainians. The more scared I was – or sounded – the better the messaging for them. I felt so sorry for my mum, but at the same time I was an animal caught in an iron trap. The only thing I could do was howl with pain. That said, at least some of the time, I picked up little pieces of information that could be cheering. My complicity with their bullshit bought me some news from home. It was from Mum I heard that Diana had left Mykolaiv, because it was being heavily shelled, for the safety of Hungary and that, later, she had made it to Blighty. This was a huge relief to me. Mum would also tell me that she was making progress, that she was in regular contact with the Foreign Office. It was cheering to hear that back in Britain the wheels were turning. But would they move fast enough?

The call that took me aback was when Popov dialled a number and a Welsh woman's voice came on the line. The reception wasn't great so I couldn't make out what she was saying. I went straight into my patter: 'I am a British prisoner of war held captive in the Donetsk region in eastern Ukraine and the authorities here . . .'

The lady at the other end cut in: '. . . sorry, caller, what is the long number at the top of the form . . .'

'. . . They want to trade me for Viktor Medvedchuk . . .'

'. . . What is your 11-digit V5C reference number, please? . . .'

'. . . I'm a prisoner of war . . .'

'. . . or you could give me the licence-plate number of your vehicle . . .'

'. . . I was captured by the Russian army . . .'

'. . . I'm sorry about that love, but unless you give the 11-digit number . . .'

'. . . What is this place? . . .'

'. . . It's the DVLA, love . . .'

'. . . What? . . .'

'. . . The Driver and Vehicle Licensing Agency, love . . .'

'. . . I think someone has called the wrong number.'

My best explanation for Popov's mistake is that being a secret-police press officer, he thought any British government body with three or four initials must do sinister work. It was funny, but the thought of being in the hands of these morons got me down.

Their next trick was that they wanted me to open a YouTube channel in my own name, which would be used to humiliate me further and press home Russian talking points, that the Ukrainians are all Nazis and so on, while maintaining the illusion that I was somehow free to talk.

The thought of refusing to comply at this point was beyond me. I had already seen what happened to those who tried to maintain their pride and, at this point, I was broken. It wasn't about them exploring the limits of my courage but me plumbing the depths of my cowardice. When would I hit bottom? For the moment I was still going deeper, deeper, always down.

The propaganda was relentless, industrial, nonsensical. Any honest viewer of these wretched videos could track back to before I had surrendered, to see a British man fighting with the Ukrainian Marines, unscarred and contemptuous of the Russian story that they were fighting Nazis. Two days later up I pop, my face smashed in, spouting Kremlin script lines. Still, they had me under their control and they would come to me day after day. None of it was live. They always got to review what had been said before they pressed publish. I had heard how back in Stalin's time prisoners were sentenced to 'ten years without rights of communication' – that meant they would be shot but that their families would not know that their loved one was dead. To tweak the agony of loss and to heighten control over the corpse's family and friends, some prisoners about to be shot were made to write a series of letters, dated into the future. Long after they had been shot, their loved ones would receive letters from a decomposing corpse. I felt trapped in the same ghastly web.

On dozens of occasions, our prison routine was disrupted when we heard the signature sound of a grad volley being fired from close to us. They had driven the grad artillery truck to the street outside the prison and fired at the Ukrainian side and zoomed off, sharpish. The trick was to hope for retaliatory fire which might well kill some of us – and so the Russians would have an atrocity to show-case for their propaganda. Boy, would I have liked to tell that story. But, of course, I dared not. It would have been pointless – and my death sentence.

One morning a UBOP goon opened the cell door and barked: 'Johnny Rambo! Come here!' You can get a feel for my mental state that I felt terrified leaving the cock-roaches, the lice, and the hot stink of my fellow prisoners, not knowing what treats my captors had in store for me. The goon took me out into the hallway where the recep-tion was, and from there into a side room where I had my fingerprints and some photos taken using the same stand-ard sort of kit you would see down your local nick after a night out having drunk too much and disturbed the neigh-bourhood. We spent around thirty minutes getting everything scanned. I still didn't get the gist of what was happening.

Another goon rocked up, cuffed me, hands in front – the polite way – and led me outside the front door of UBOP where I came across my new custodian. He was short, around five foot six inches, sporting a T-shirt embla-zoned with the letter Z on it. Let's call him Tweedle-Z. He led me through a series of fences to the street outside. I was still in the dark as to what was happening, but it was great to check out of Hotel California. If that was what was going on: once again, the not knowing added to my chronic fear. We walked across a cobblestone street and tram tracks, the tram that we could hear but not see from our cell. Tweedle-Z had a colleague sitting in a little Lada, who was, who could only be, Tweedle-Y.

Was this the exchange? My hopes went on a big dipper, soaring, then plunging. As per the rules of UBOP, I kept my head bowed during the whole trip but used the sides of my eyes to peer out from the back seat of the Lada – the other stooge sat beside me – to gaze at the big bad world of Donetsk. For a prisoner, trapped in a square box with no natural light for weeks on end, it was like an acid trip: bowling along in daylight, seeing ordinary people going shopping, chatting, a beautiful woman sitting at a pavement cafe: it was all so exciting.

But where were we going? What were they going to do to me next? We pulled up in front of a large, imposing building, got out and walked towards a door which, to my fevered imagination, led to a basement. I feared I was going to be tortured again, but the good news was that the stooge hit a lift button and we went up, not down. My heart skipped a beat.

We got to the third floor and he pressed a buzzer. An old gentleman walking with a cane opened the door and let us in. Tweedle-Z disappeared somewhere while the old guy walked Tweedle-Y and me through a little office room to his grander suite where he offered me a seat and asked me, in a very soft, educated voice, if I wanted tea or coffee. I was gobsmacked. Used to the dark mood at UBOP, a little touch of civility felt like meeting a space alien. I answered yes to coffee and a young blonde woman appeared – I guessed she was his PA – and made us both coffee and brought us biscuits. I had been living on one chunk of bread a day, half the size of my fist, so the idea of biscuits was troubling.

I had had so little to eat and evacuating your bowels in UBOP was so problematic I had not done a number two for the three weeks I had been there. Call me Mr Constipation. I became worried that if I ate a biscuit it might cause me to go. I didn't know if I was going back to Hotel California. The old guy said in Russian: 'We are just waiting for your translator.'

I drank the coffee. I ate some biscuits. It felt like a banquet.

After twenty minutes Tweedle-Z told me to follow him. Again, I was still troubled because there was only him and me and, even though I was handcuffed, he was so little I could still have taken him out. But I guess he figured that if I managed to escape, I would still be stuck in the dead centre of Donetsk. We climbed up the stairwell and ended up on the top floor in an office suite smaller and less distinguished than the old guy's. Shortly, the translator I had come across in UBOP turned up, trailing her Soviet perfume, along with a short, fat guy in a white shirt and sporting a scruffy beard who seemed to have come along for the laughs.

The translator finally let me know what was happening: 'Today you are going to be charged.' The charge sheet went on a bit: they hit me with forcible seizure of power, forcible retention of power, planning to overthrow the Constitution of the Donetsk People's Republic, being a mercenary and killing civilians.

But who was who? Tweedle-Z was the investigating

prosecutor, the translator explained, then she turned to the short fat guy in the white shirt with the scruffy beard and said he was my defence lawyer. His name was Pavel Kosovan. At no time did I see Kosovan away from the goons. There was no confidential legal advice, no proper independent legal process. As to Kosovan, from the get-go I had the feeling that he was utterly useless. Good intuition. It turned out that he was a nasty little crook who tried to stiff my mum for a ton of money. But that was down the track.

Kosovan offered me a cigarette and I instantly accepted, not knowing where my next fag would come from. While I waited, Tweedle-Z turned to the translator and told her what the plan was. They were going to read out the charges and I would plead guilty to all of them. The charge that I did not like one little bit was that I had killed civilians. I knew what they were trying to do, they were trying to paint me as the big bad wolf, in the same way they had made me wear the Azov T-shirt.

A guy with a jacket saying RT – Russia's patsy media station – turned up with a camera and tripod, set it up, and I was filmed as they read out the charges. I acknowledged serving in the Ukrainian military, but I flat out refused to say on camera – or off it, for that matter – that I had killed civilians. Whatever they did to me, I wasn't saying I had killed civilians. I had not done that. I had not done the other things too, but saying I had killed civilians would have been a breach of my honour as a soldier. I had finally stopped diving and hit the limit of my cowardice.

I had found bottom.

The camera switched off. Do it properly, they said. The camera switched on. When they got to 'Do you plead guilty to killing civilians?', again I said 'I'm not saying that.' Off and on, the camera went, off and on, until they gave up. I pleaded guilty to a lot of rubbish but not to killing civilians. What I had not realized was that I had been tricked because they had withheld the awful consequence of something I had pleaded guilty to. It was a dark thing to do, but it was only much later that I began to work out how the trick they had played on me would work.

Propaganda video in the bag, I asked my lawyer if I could use the loo. I needed to poo badly because the last time I had been was the morning before we surrendered. But when I got into the cubicle it felt like I was having to move heaven and earth. Eventually, what felt like a small planet – Pluto, maybe – shifted. Like life, constipation comes at you hard. What had felt like the biggest piece of shit in the solar system – the whole fucking galaxy, frankly – turned out to be a small, dark pebble. To be fair, I hadn't eaten anything other than a little piece of bread once a day for the past three weeks.

Relieved, but not really willing to share why with my captors, I went outside to find the investigator, Tweedle-Z. He told me that they were going to X-ray me in hospital. I wasn't going for a medical check-up or for them to treat my stab wound but simply to ensure that I did not have TB. If I was in the clear, they would take me out of UBOP to somewhere else.

We went downstairs, got in the Lada, and drove for about twenty minutes across town until we reached

Donetsk Hospital. I had seen better-run hospitals in Kurdish-controlled Syria and that is saying something. After a lot of faffing around, Tweedle-Z and Tweedle-Y managed to find where the radiography department was. The X-ray machine was so antique it looked like it had been bought at a knock-down price from a fire sale of the stage set from the *Chernobyl* TV series. After I had been irradiated with God knows how many gamma rays, we got back in the Lada for another magical mystery tour of Donetsk.

We pulled up outside a police holding tank, in Russian Изолятор Временного Содержания, ИВС or EVS for short, which in English stands for Temporary Detention Facility. Tweedle-Z opened the door for me, I got out, and we hurried over to the steps of the building. It was late, well past nine o'clock, and the street was pretty dark apart from the feeble glow thrown by some street lamps, so I didn't get a good look but I could tell the building as a whole had seen better days. As we walked up the stairs, the doors buzzed open and we entered a cage. Only when the cage door behind us closed did the door ahead open. We were met with another set of gates, walked through them, down a set of stairs into a courtyard where one corner was given over to a pen of guard dogs that started barking madly at us. How to describe them? They didn't look like the puppies in the bog-roll ads, to put it mildly. If some sick psycho wanted to create an image of an unfriendly place, then they had done very well. The EVS, run-down as it was, was secure with a capital S.

Some guards appeared out of the gloom and a voice

asked who was their new guest. Tweedle-Z explained that
I was 'a British mercenary' and one of the goons, built
like a brick outhouse in blue camo uniform, asked me
whether I wanted to see his Putin tattoo. It seemed impol-
ite to say no, so I put on a neutral impression as he bared
his chest and there was the Master of the Kremlin astride
this bloke's nipples. Putin Tits barked some gibberish at me
while I practised my deadpan. Tweedle-Z led the way into
a room that looked like your standard custody suite at any
police station and, to be honest, rather well kept. I got
booked in and Tweedle-Z said all I had on me was a pack
of cigarettes – he left out the bit about him giving them to
me in the car. Then he left and my anxiety levels went
through the roof.

Two guards told me to follow them, and I was dreading
what was going to happen next. I followed them head
down, hands behind my back. They took me to an empty
room, similar to the place where I had been beaten sense-
less in UBOP. One of the guards told me to undress. I
stripped down to my boxers but then he said take everything off, so I whipped them off too. He rifled through my
clothes to double-check that I had nothing hidden and
then he told me to bend over. Back in the steelworks when
we were preparing for surrender, I had toyed with hiding
a small SD card up my arse. Lord knows what would have
happened had I done so. The guard duly looked up at
where the sun does not shine. I understand that in any
society, prisons are necessary to place evildoers where they
belong, but I have always wondered: why become a screw?
To look up other people's arses? I don't get it.

My arse inspected, another guard in slippers shuffled in. He was so laid-back, so unbothered, I was left with the feeling that he wasn't that fussed about what he was doing for a living. I followed him up two flights of stairs before reaching a set of gates. There, he gestured for me to turn to face the wall while he opened the gate and then we came to a corridor of cell doors much like you would see in a British prison. The screw in slippers unlocked the cell door, swung it open. I walked in and then he locked it behind me. For all my foreboding, EVS was a cut above UBOP. The cell was relatively big with five beds, a sink, a toilet, a wooden floor, and heated somehow. In the corner of the room was a large window with reinforced glass protected by iron bars. Still, it let in natural light. My new cellmates went out of their way to be pleasant. They quickly worked out that I was British, reassured me that EVS was OK – 'they don't beat you here'. I can't remember their names, but three were Ukrainian Red Cross volunteers who had been delivering aid to Mariupol when they got trapped in the siege, the fourth had been some kind of security guy at Mariupol port and the fifth a petty criminal, but nice enough.

'Are you hungry?' asked one of the Red Cross volunteers. I said yes and the petty criminal offered me some bread that he had saved. Not knowing the score in EVS, I said: 'No, I can't take your bread.' But then they told me they were being fed three times a day: breakfast, lunch and dinner, nothing spectacular but so much better than the à la carte menu at UBOP. I wolfed what the criminal gave me, half a loaf of brown bread. The guys told me that the water was drinkable, so I got an empty bottle, filled it up at the tap, and drained two bottles' worth in quick succession.

The one negative was that there was a camera on the ceiling, observing everything we were doing. Big Brother was watching. Yeah, whatever. Natural light, food, water, a toilet, some space: it felt like I had rocked up at a boutique hotel.

The leader of the Red Cross volunteers was a kindly soul, an old gentleman with a beard whom I shall call Andrei. It was time for bed and they gave me some blankets to make a makeshift mattress. I set up my bed on the floor under the table and so out of sight of Big Brother.

The moment I closed my eyes I was dead to the world.

At six o'clock in the morning a guard came and knocked on the door and called out our names. At each name, we would run up to the peep-eye window so that he could check and then he moved on to the next cell. Then came the dinner lady, handing out a bit of porridge in a metal bowl: not great, not terrible. I hoovered that down, then washed my bowl so that I could give it back to the dinner lady.

I spent most of my time in EVS sleeping and washing and using the toilet – oh! It was luxury. After six wonderful nights, Andrei, the old hand, got word that I was going to be moved again. My anxiety attacks started anew. The next day we woke up, did roll-call, and I was waiting for breakfast when the guard came to the door and told me to get ready to leave. I was led back down to the processing area and met by some male transport guards and a young female guard. She was something of a tomboy and when I appeared she exclaimed in English: 'Oh, Mortarman!' She told me to follow her and I traipsed behind to the court-yard holding the dog pen.

There was something not quite right about Tomboy. She wasn't horrible or abusive but weirdly overexcited. While we hung out, waiting for other prisoners to be collected and my paperwork to be checked, she seemed like she was off her head on something. After a lot of faffing around, they finally found the last of the five prisoners who they were moving that day and we trooped out to the paddy wagon (police van) that was going to take us to the big prison, a place that is still the backdrop to some of my darkest nightmares.

## CHAPTER TWELVE

# Murder on Death Row

The doors of the paddy wagon slammed shut. It was a largish van containing two narrow cages, one down the driver's side, the other down the passenger's side. There were six of us, Ukrainian prisoners of war from different units, three in each cage. We knew the rules. No talking but a certain, sly exchange of looks between the aristocracy of human souls who find themselves on the wrong side of the law in a place where the law doesn't mean very much. In my cage was an old guy in his fifties – let's call him Gramps – wearing smart, grandad-style clothes and good shoes, as if he had been going out somewhere nice before he'd fallen out with what passed for law and order in the DPR. A second guy was younger, injured in some way and on crutches. The others were Ukrainian soldiers but not from the marines. The van started up and moved forward slightly. The main gate to EVS clanked open and we drove for ten minutes, less, when we slowed down. I heard what sounded like big prison gates swing open and the van drove on into some kind of courtyard.

We had entered the Donetsk SIZO – СИЗО, short for Следственный Изолятор – a pretrial detention centre. It was a special kind of hell. The first SIZO in the city was built in 1911 when Donetsk was called Hughesovka, named after the Welsh mining engineer John Hughes, who founded the city in 1869 for the then tsar. Hughes hired sixty oxen to drag an iron furnace on a giant sleigh across the frozen wastes to exploit the iron and coal seams in the Donbas. After the 1917 revolution, the Communists renamed Hughesovka Stalino, and when the truth started to dawn about that old monster, Donetsk. The prison was destroyed during the Second World War but rebuilt in the 1950s – and the foul atmosphere of Stalin's time still lingered.

As the doors of the van were opened, the guards started barking at us 'Quickly! Quickly!' in Russian. We tumbled out of our cages and clattered down a flight of stairs. Then more shouts, we had to turn back and help the prisoner on crutches hobble down the steps into the basement processing area, lined with walls painted blue and blue ceramic tiles on the floor. They told us to line up and as we did so the slightly crackpot tomboy guard appeared, said 'Hello, Mortarman!' and told the other guards that I was a British mercenary. That didn't lighten the mood.

One of them barked at me: 'Ah Hollywood! I have seen you on TV. Do you like to box?' He was a real bruiser, very well-built and in far better nick than me. I hastily ducked the challenge, but he gave me a long stare, suggesting that he wanted to beat the shit out of me.

Tomboy was up to her old tricks, goading him: 'Have you seen Mortarman's tattoo? He's got a trident' – the symbol of the Ukrainian army – 'on his left arm.' Helpfully – or, in fact, not helpfully at all – she quickly took my arm and lifted the sleeve to show him. Bruiser smiled and asked, 'Would you like me to remove it?', gesturing that he would do so by peeling the skin off with a knife.

Another guard called me forward and I went to the custody suite to be processed. In charge of that was a young female prison guard, quite attractive to be honest, who took my fingerprints and then told me to remove my shirt so that photos could be taken of my tattoos. The eroticism of that moment was rather enjoyable – but short-lived. Next, we were checked by the prison doctor. He measured our height and took blood samples to check for HIV. Then five of us, minus the prisoner on crutches, were squeezed into a tiny holding cell. When I say tiny, I mean tiny: it was built to hold one or two people at the most, and we were crammed in there.

After maybe two hours the door opened and they summoned the first three prisoners by name, one by one. They tied a blue cotton hood over their heads. The cell door closed and was locked, leaving just two of us, listening to what was going to happen next.

The guards shouted at the three prisoners to lay down. They then asked them what unit they had served in. '53rd Mechanized Brigade,' they each replied. The bad news is that the 53rd was the receiving unit for soldiers of the disbanded and disgraced far-right unit, the Aidar Battalion, who the Russians and their proxies hated with a passion. The Ukrainian government had shut down the Aidar Battalion for its serial breaches of the rules of war.

We then heard 'Blyat!', best translated as 'Fuck you!'

The guards started clubbing their prone, hooded, defenceless captives with their truncheons. The cell was just a temporary construction, so the only thing separating the middle-aged fellow and myself from the screams of agony was a thin sheet of metal. There are few things more grotesquely horrible in life than listening to people being tortured and howling in pain a few feet from you – and not being able to do anything about it.

After a time, the guards varied their game. They made their poor captives crawl along the corridor, beating them all the while. They called this 'running the gauntlet'. Hooded, knocked about, the prisoners kept bashing their heads into the walls or going the wrong way, bringing on a fresh hail of blows. Trapped in our tiny cell, Gramps and I could not of course see any of this. It was like listening to an evil radio play, our imaginations working overtime. The old chap crossed himself according to the Christian Orthodox tradition, bringing the tips of his thumb, index and middle fingers together, the ring and little fingers pressed against his palm. He, too, was afraid.

The screams subsided. In the distance, a cell door opened and was slammed shut, then locked. Footsteps came towards our cell, then stopped.

'Aslin!'

'Yes, sir!'

'Come here!'

The door swung open and a guard tied a blue hood over my head.

'Do you understand Russian?'

'Yes, sir.'

'Lie down!'

I dropped to the floor quicker than I could say go. The guard started laying into me, although it was not as bad as I thought it might be: the dentist's waiting-room effect in play, again. He was whacking my bottom with his truncheon, yelling at me to crawl. Sightless, I did my best to speed out of the cell and along the corridor as fast as possible.

'Go down the stairs!'

My hands groped for the first step and then I lunged forward, almost tumbling in my desperation to avoid his truncheon. I had no idea how long the flight of stairs was and smashed my head into something metallic – a landing, a side door, I had no idea – cutting my forehead. Now I was trapped, my head against the object, my legs still on the stairs, the guard still whacking me on my bottom, more viciously than before.

I remember thinking: 'Is this it?' Was this how my life was going to end?

It is absolutely true to say that I was scared shitless. But then the thought occurred to me, in, I think, a very British way: 'It's a good thing that I'm into BDSM.' I can't explain why the thought popped into my head, but once there it was hard to displace it. I could end up oh so very dead, but inside my head I was having a bit of a giggle.

My hands reached the base of the steps and the guard yelled: 'Forward!'

I groped along for a metre and then hit another set of stairs.

'Up the stairs!'

I have no idea of the route I had taken but I must have gone seventy metres up, down, around and around, sightless and beaten continually before the guard got bored with the torture. I reached the top of some stairs and the guard ordered me to stand. I staggered upright, wary of toppling back down. The guard locked his arms around my left arm, bent my head down and pushed me along, through some gates, and I now smelt, from the stink of too much humanity held in close proximity, that I was inside the cell block. A door opened and a bright light shone through the hood.

The guard ripped the hood off and pushed me inside, yelling: 'Lie down!'

I quickly ran in and lay face down on the concrete floor.

'The rules are: 10 p.m., sleep; 6 a.m., wake up; you learn the Russian national anthem. If you don't, we will fuck you! It is forbidden to sit down. If you are caught, you will be punished. Johnny, you understand?'

'Yes sir!'

The cell door slammed shut. I stood up and dusted myself off. When I recovered, I looked round at the other guys: Gramps, who, it turned out, was a retired captain in the Ukrainian army; Bohdan, in his early forties and like me a marine in my battalion; and Maksym, a young National Guard soldier. There were four of us in a cell designed for two; two bunks with some battered, dirty mattresses that had seen better days, no pillows, no blankets. But a toilet and a sink with drinking water were at least some comfort. The cell boasted a window looking out on to a side bit of the prison. It had no glass, so that we were exposed to the elements. However, at least we had some natural light. In my experience, older prisons are more humane than newer ones.

After the hideous welcome committee we had just endured, what came next was fucking weird. A Tannoy placed near the vent shaft just above the door started playing classical music.

'They are torturing us with Mozart,' I joked.

High up on the wall was a photograph of Vladimir Putin, the Lord God of everything in this stinking hellhole. I imagined there would once have been prisoners of the Nazis in awful places like this who had to look up at a photo of Adolf Hitler. Beneath Putin were the words of the Russian anthem printed out on a sheet of A4. Before I could pay attention to learning them, we heard one of the guards yell to the trustee who was wheeling along the food trolley outside. In Russian prison slang they call him the 'balandyor'. Then we heard the clattering of a large pan being lifted. There was a slot built into the cast-iron door that swivelled like a tray. The trustee called for our two bowls which were stacked by the sink. We passed them along and put them on the swivel tray and pushed it so that the trustee, on the other side of the door, dolloped the food into them and then pushed it back: mashed potato in one bowl, some boiled fish in the other. The others got stuck in, but I wasn't keen, fearing that we would get beaten up again and I didn't want to throw up, so they had my portion too.

After our beating, we were all scared to sit down on the bunks so we stood, hour after hour. The problem was that all our watches and phones had been taken from us, so although we knew it was pitch-black outside, we had no idea whether it was 10 p.m. yet – and safe to hit the sack. To add to our anxiety, every now and then a guard would walk by and, sometimes but not always, he would lift the peephole to check up on us.

Gramps, Maks and Bohdan had had enough. They wanted to sleep, but I was super-uneasy, fearing another beating. The bunks were narrow and only really suitable for one person. Bohdan and Maks jumped on to the top bunk – there was no ladder – and tried to position themselves so they could lay down, head-to-toe, toe-to-head. Gramps and I did the same, but I couldn't settle and told them: 'This isn't right.' Out in the corridor something moved, so we all jumped and stood, utterly exhausted, for another hour before a guard came along and told us we could sleep.

Sadism has its own etiquette, as does a posh dinner party. If you don't follow the rules, then things will not go well for you. When a guard shouted that he was about to open the door, we all had to say: '*Slava Rossiya! Slava Rossiya! Slava Rossiya! Akhmat Sila! Donbas Sila!*' – 'Glory to Russia!' three times. Akhmat/Akhmad was the father of the pro-Putin Chechen quisling Ramzan Kadyrov, '*Sila*' means strong, so we were intoning 'Akhmat is strong! Donbas is strong!' (It should be noted, with some irony, that Akhmad

Kadyrov had been assassinated in a bomb blast by Chechen Islamists in Grozny during a Victory Day memorial parade in May 2004.) We had to lie face down on the floor so there was zero chance that we could attack our captors. If we didn't lie doggo, we would get beaten. When we were moved from the cell to somewhere else in the prison, we were hooded and we had to move with our heads, necks and backs bent forward at 45 degrees, our faces almost in our knees, our hands behind our back. In the Russian prison system they call this the 'black dolphin'.

The worst guard was a psychopath. Mr Mackay from *Porridge*, the great BBC sitcom about life in a British prison, was all sweetness and light compared to the man we nicknamed Three Four, in Russian, Три Четыре – tri chetyre. When I was doing the black dolphin – blindfolded by the hood, head bent low, arms behind my back – Three Four would deliberately guide me so that my head bashed into the prison's heavy iron doors. He got his nickname because every time he came on shift he would shout 'You're all fucked!' in Russian and then 'Three Four', missing out the 'One Two' for some reason, probably because he was a moron. On the 'Three Four' command we had to start singing the Russian national anthem. It's a fucking awful tune and I hate it. Once he made us sing it non-stop from the start of his shift at 7 a.m. up to 6 p.m. when a different guard, Mr Vera, came on duty. He in turn earned his nickname because he would play Radio Vera all day long. 'Vera' is Russian for 'faith' and Radio Vera is a Russian Orthodox Christian music station which plays hymns, choral and classical music. The other senior guard we called

Mr Khorosho – Russian for 'good' – because he was a bit of a sweetie, very much like Mr Barrowclough in *Porridge*. He also said 'khorosho' in a pleasant manner and was pretty much nice to everyone, prisoners and fellow guards alike, so very different from Three Four. Out of all the guards Mr Khorosho was probably the only one who just wanted to do his job and never tried to humiliate us.

Learning the Russian national anthem by heart was a torture all by itself. As the lyrics were copied out on paper directly underneath our cell's photograph of Putin, we had no excuse not to learn them. For hour after hour we practised singing them, but I was never, ever word-perfect.

On the second day in SIZO, Maks was called out and disappeared from our lives, to be replaced by Viktor. We all got on with each other well, but I built up a particular friendship with Bohdan. He helped me learn the anthem, but I was a terrible pupil, only picking up the first three lines that first evening. Bohdan had been in my marine battalion, second or third in command, and I had seen him around in the steelworks, but we had never worked together in a unit. We soon became good friends, almost family. Prison is funny like that: the intensity of being locked up makes you almost fall in love with some people, and others you can end up hating so much you almost want to kill them.

The other three had all been officers so Bohdan's favourite joke was to pull rank and remind me that I was just a simple private – as if, in that place, rank mattered a damn. And he got a lot of laughs out of my great struggle with the fucking Russian anthem. Getting to know all the words was a source of great stress to me because I am dyslexic. I could understand some Russian but I couldn't pronounce the words correctly or retain the sequence of phrases for longer than a goldfish. Worse, the guards insisted that I recite the words – not sing them – so I was robbed of the crutch of melody to guide me. Again and again, I would get the words wrong. Or I would do an Eric Morecambe when he performed Grieg's Piano Concerto with 'Andre Preview': getting all the right notes – words in my case – 'but not necessarily in the right order'.

The stress grew worse when I realized that learning the Russian anthem was a favourite method of the guards to beat up new prisoners. On our wing, we would hear new arrivals being ordered to sing the anthem. Of course, most Ukrainian soldiers would have no idea of the words. As they stuttered into silence, the guards would open their cell door and take out the unfortunate newbie for a beating. I was always on edge, spending every minute staring at the piece of paper on the wall. The first verse went like this:

> Russia is our sacred power,
> Россия – священная наша держава,
> Russia is our beloved country.
> Россия – любимая наша страна.
> Mighty will, great glory –
> Могучая воля, великая слава –
> Yours for ever!
> Твое достоянье на все времена!
> Hail, our free Fatherland!
> Славься, Отечество наше свободное!

I remember that I dared to ask Viktor what would happen if I didn't learn it and he said: 'They will fuck us all.' But he was joking. In the end it took me a whole fortnight to learn the full anthem. One day the guard turned up and it was my turn to sing it. I gave it everything I had and the guard listened, then walked off without rebuking me.

The moment the coast was clear Viktor burst out laughing. The bit where I was supposed to have sung 'protected by God, Our native land', I had actually come out with 'limping by God, Our vulnerable land.'

How I hated that fucking song.

One morning the cell door opened and we saw the senior warden smiling at us with a small video camera in his hand. We all stood up, feeling uneasy. I didn't know whether to smile back but I am glad I didn't. He turned the camera on and asked each of us in turn whether we had been well treated.

'Tak, tochno' – Yes, boss – we lied in perfect harmony. Then he left.

I had a sense that something was up. Did the warden's filming prefigure the big exchange I had been dreaming about? I was about to find out. My name was called, the cell door opened, but then the guard ordered the other three to leave. We were being split up and we had no time to say our goodbyes. There was a lot of commotion going on, the sounds of a lot of prisoners moving from their cells – perhaps, I dared to hope – to be exchanged. But after a short while it became obvious that the news for me was bad. I wasn't going anywhere, probably because I was, in their eyes, a high-value prisoner. I felt a wall of depression hit me and wanted to burst into tears. Somehow, I held myself together.

They led me to another cell on the same wing. Shortly afterwards the senior warden popped by, again with camera in hand, and said in his broken English: 'Johnny, this is your new camera.'

He meant cell. I didn't bother to correct his English.

As with all the better dinner parties, introductions in Russian-run prisons are all-important. I introduced myself to my new cellmates as 'Johnny' – Aiden still being a challenge to pronounce – and we all shook hands. Vova, fluent in English, was in his late thirties and had been in the army; Roma was a soldier of roughly the same age; and Leo, in his late twenties, was a captain. They were all dying to find out how on earth an Englishman had ended up in the Donetsk. Vova was one of the brave lads who had tried to make it out from the siege of Mariupol some 140 kilometres to Ukrainian lines. He had done well and walked a long way north for eight days when on March 20th he stumbled into a passing group of Russian infantry soldiers. They beat him up, before feeding him into the DPR legal system, if that is what it was. We speculated a lot about what the big movement of people meant. Our deduction was that the DPR bosses and the Kremlin above them were holding on to high-value prisoners but trading the lower ranks and lesser fry. That conclusion deepened my depression, but we hoped there might be another exchange in the following month.

We chatted a bit about *fenya* – Russian prison slang. Essentially, Russian criminals have developed a private language for themselves to keep their guards guessing. The authorities keep on trying to ban it, to no avail. Back in the day, *fenya* had a lot of Greek loanwords, then Georgian, then Yiddish and Hebrew. Fun words include 'pedal' for mobile phone, 'template' for military headgear, and 'para-sha', literally meaning a slop bucket or an open toilet, but used to describe prisoners of the lowest rank who end up sleeping next to the bog. The sense of humour in *fenya* is anthracite black: 'Oh, I forgot to tell you: your wife died this spring.'

Dinner time was upon us. The older guys ate first, sitting down on two small stools while the younger ones – Leo and I – squatted on the floor waiting for them to finish their share. We listened to the news blasted out via the prison Tannoy system. Often, it was just Kremlin rubbish but occasionally it broke genuine news. Suddenly I heard my name and those of Shaun Pinner and Brahim Saâdoune, a Moroccan lad who was also in the Ukrainian Marines. The breaking news was that our trial for being mercenaries was coming to court soon. I felt my throat run dry. Anxiety, no, worse, dread gripped hold of me.

The news also reported that the Azov Battalion had just surrendered. One of us said: 'They are in for a fun time.' It was a joke – but not a funny one.

Anyone in the Azov Battalion or affiliated to it was given a horrible time. One guy in a unit connected to Azov turned up in my cell. Dima – let's call him – was a proud Ukrainian patriot and strong, mentally and physically. The guards sensed that and turned up the dial on their sadism. When he ran the gauntlet, he was beaten even more excessively than usual. The guards would not let him sleep on the mattress but made him lie on the bare floor, with no blanket even, like a dog. In the week or two that followed, the guards would come in and beat him on his hands, Adam's apple, face and genitals with their police truncheons. I witnessed this with my own eyes. We were not supposed to look and were forced to lie face down, but I could see what they were doing out of the corners of my eyes. Once, they told him to spread his legs and beat him on his genitals. The guards told him that they would beat him for sixty-two days because he was 'a Nazi'. I had no idea what 'sixty-two days' signified in their mind. Dima got moved to another cell. Over the coming days eight more people from his unit arrived in SIZO and they, too, were treated brutally.

But what happened to Dima wasn't the darkest event I experienced in my time in SIZO.

It happened around seven o'clock in the evening, when Mr Khorosho had been on shift. We always liked it when he was the boss: we didn't have to sing the fucking anthem all the time and we could sit on the bunks without too much worry. It started like it always started: the sound of screaming, screams echoing down the corridor from the processing area that led to our cell block. It's something I won't be able to forget. This time, the screams went on for a lot longer than they normally do. Perhaps this poor fellow was, like Dima, affiliated to Azov, or even in Azov itself.

Remember, all my friends in my cell, in fact, virtually every person in that prison, had screamed themselves. We knew what it was like to be blindfolded by the hood, to crawl along the floor, and down and up the stairs while being clobbered constantly by a truncheon.

His agony was ours too.

It didn't stop. As the poor man got closer to our cell block, the screams grew more piercing, more hideous, more unhuman. By this time, after UBOP and now SIZO, I had – kind of – been proud of the fact that I could go numb, that I was no longer that bothered by suffering. Not with this man, screaming so piteously.

The victim was close, so close that we expected our cell door to swing open. Instead, the door of the next cell along opened. The beating stopped and we heard the guard shout 'Lie down!' He then explained the prison rules and asked the prisoner what his position was. The voice of the prisoner was too weak for us to hear it, but the guard repeated it out loud: 'Tanker!'

Then we heard him hit his victim again.

'Do you understand, *blyat*?'

Then he hit him again.

'*Blyat*, are you sleeping?'

We heard the sound of him beating someone, but this time there were no screams, no grunts, not even a mew of pain. It was just the sound of a truncheon clubbing a body.

The clubbing sound stopped.

The guard told the other cellmates to clean him up, the cell door closed, and we heard the guard's steps fall away. We could hear the others in the cell speaking but not loud enough for us to understand. We sat down, our faces grim, grimmer than before. What had we just listened to? It was almost as if we already knew what had happened or was about to happen. But none of us dared say that word.

The unspoken rule in the SIZO was never, ever seek to attract the attention of the guards. Or else.

So I felt sick with fear when those in the next cell started banging on their door, then shouting, then going to the window and shouting to guards walking along outside in the courtyard. They were shouting: 'Medic! We need a medic.'

Steps, someone moving fast.

'What's the problem?' The voice of Mr Khorosho.

And then we heard one of them say: 'He's stopped breathing. We are doing CPR on him, but he needs a medic.'

'OK,' said Mr Khorosho. Then he left.

Ten, fifteen minutes passed. The voice of the woman doctor outside the next cell was clear: 'What happened?' We could not make out what the prisoners replied. They spoke softly for a reason.

'Keep on doing the CPR.' Then she asked the guards to open the door.

They opened the door and we heard the other prisoners leave the cell.

Then the medic gave the time of death, the only medical attention the prisoner had received.

He had been in the custody of SIZO for no longer than one hour, and now he was dead.

The four of us stood in silence, not daring to look at each other, not daring to speak, not daring to breathe.

## CHAPTER THIRTEEN

# Wicked Game

One morning, steps outside our cell.

'Lie down!'

We hit the floor.

The door was unlocked.

'Aslin! Stand up!'

'*Slava Rossiya! Slava Rossiya! Slava Rossiya! Akhmat Sila! Donbas Sila!*'

I walked over to the door, head bowed, arms stretched in the black dolphin position behind my back. They hand-cuffed and hooded me and led me through the processing area, past the route they normally took when I had to do propaganda bullshit. So wherever I was going, this was something new. I was made to stand against a wall while the guards, never the brightest of people, figured out what they had to figure out. Then a new guard appeared, removed my hood and led me out, through a series of gates, into the courtyard. They put me in the back of a little minibus while they waited for another prisoner to be fetched. Then the escort guards jumped in and we were off, through the main prison gate. The drive lasted five minutes, if that. Wherever we had arrived now wasn't a prison and it didn't have a bad vibe about it. A middle-aged woman in a doctor's white coat appeared and behind her some heart-pump monitors and that kind of malarkey. I thought: Hospital? It's a big building with sick people in it, but that's not important right now, as the joke goes in *Airplane*. She took our blood pressure and checked our signs of life – we were fine – then we were led up a set of stairs into a corridor and there, in front of us, was a cage. So perhaps we were in the courthouse. They opened the cage gate, urged me in, and I looked around.

'Hey! Johnny!' It was Brahim, the Moroccan lad. 'Good to see you man, how you been?'

'Shut up!' I whispered to him.

'It's OK. They can't hurt us here,' he hit back.

He was right, but I was still traumatized by the killing in the next-door cell two days before and utterly submissive – too much so, I now realize. But the sadism of SIZO had broken me and I was in bits.

The last time I had seen Brahim was the night before we had surrendered. He was just twenty-one and had only joined the military in September 2021. He was actually in the same company as me but in a different platoon. He had not surrendered when I had, instead he hung out in the steelworks for a couple of days. Then, faced with next to no food and no ammo, he surrendered.

'What is this place?' I whispered.

'It's the health commission, to see if we are fit for court.'

'Where's Shaun?'

'He's seeing the psychologist.'

What was weird about the DPR is that they had all the semblance of a proper justice system, yet it was all a shadow play. The real thing was the sound of a truncheon hitting a body.

Brahim and Shaun were being held in a black site, a secret prison with a truly grim reputation. I don't know for sure why I didn't end up there but I suspect that it was because they were using me for their propaganda games, so they wanted to place me inside their formal prison system, dark as it was. I told Brahim I was in SIZO with other Ukrainian POWs.

'Do you get beaten there?' I tried to keep my voice as quiet as possible.

'Yes. And you?'

I held my tongue.

'Is our commander still alive?' he continued.

Brahim was referring to one of our guys. I told him he was still with us, then he mumbled something about the second in command of our company being dead. He then turned to the other POW sitting on his other side, who was from the 501st Marine Battalion. They had surrendered a week before we did but their action had critically weakened our positions to the east of the steelworks, and this was a bone of contention between his battalion and ours.

'Why did you lot surrender?' Brahim asked him.

'We were taking heavy casualties and ran out of food

and ammo . . .' the other guy started, but then the guard got irritated with our chatter and told us to shut it. A few moments passed by and, after a nod from someone else further down the hall, he opened the gate and gestured for me to follow him. We went down the hallway to a tiny side room where the blonde translator was sitting. I said hello and someone who looked like a cheap doctor walked in. Without any explanation, he started asking me a ton of personal questions, about my childhood, upbringing, education, life story.

After his line of questions petered out, I was returned to the cage, and there was Shaun: thinner, gaunt, haggard, but still the same old Shaun.

'How are you?' I asked.

'Shit,' he replied. 'I don't think we are getting out of this one. They want to give us the death penalty.'

I was not going to disagree with him about that but passed on the good news from my mum, that a lot of people were working hard on our behalf. The guard came and opened the gate and escorted me to the psychologist's office. There were four of them, the guy who had already asked me questions about my childhood and all, a new man who boasted a moustache the spitting image of Stalin's, a woman who sat behind the desk, and the blonde translator with the awful pong perfume.

Soft questions for starters: 'How come you are here?' 'What do you think of the Russian people?' 'What are your political leanings?' I told them what they wanted to hear. On the politics question, I replied that I was a libertarian anarchist.

Stalin's Moustache went on the offensive, asking all sorts of weird questions in an aggressive tone, as if he was playing bad cop in a bad movie. The good doc would ask a wet question every now and then. After half an hour or so of good doc, bad doc, they spat me out and had a go with the guy from the 501st. Once again, all of this made me reflect on what a strange, dark place the DPR was, a nonsense state with all the form and none of the substance of the rule of law. A judgement that also goes for all of Vladimir Putin's Russia, too.

Shaun and Brahim had been taken back to their hellhole and I got to hang out in the cage for a while. The court guard seemed a decent chap and he proved it by saying, before we got into the car heading back to SIZO, would you like a cigarette? We puffed away in the courtyard, happy as Larry. When I got back to the cell, I told my mates all the news, that I had seen Shaun and Brahim, that they had been beaten up in their black-site prison but they were still very much alive. All the Ukrainian soldiers I knew were not subject to any trial but were just hanging around waiting to be exchanged. For them, our comings and goings to the courtroom were – almost – a source of entertainment. It broke the boredom.

Later that evening a guard swung by to tell me to make sure to get washed tomorrow morning because I would be leaving the cell early, at around six thirty. It was good to know they cared about my personal hygiene. I washed myself with a jug of water, soaped and rinsed up. On cue, at six thirty in the morning the guards opened the door and out I went, cuffed with my hands behind my back but only hooded until the main door of SIZO. This time I ended up in the Donetsk prosecutors' office on the third floor, the same place I had gone a month earlier. As I walked in, I saw two prisoners with black bags on their heads: Shaun and Brahim. The guard went away and I hissed: 'Shaun, is that you?'

He told me that he'd overheard what they were up to: we were all being taken to Mariupol on some kind of crazy evidence-gathering mission. Suddenly, up popped Tweedle-Z, accompanied by some other escort guards, and he placed a black plastic bag with holes in it over my head and we were off, downstairs and into two minivans. They had put Shaun and Ibrahim in the other van. From the sound of some chit-chat I was with some girls, but I had no idea who they were.

After we had been driving for about half an hour, a man sitting next to me offered me some chewing gum and asked whether being cuffed with arms behind was uncomfortable. I said yes, so he unlocked me and switched the cuffs to the front, which was way less unpleasant. We started nattering, he asked me simple questions about life in Britain. Then after something like two hours – wars destroy roads and bridges so the journey was going to be far longer than it would have been before Putin's nonsense – we pulled to a stop. We got out and the kind man pulled the bag off my head. Up rocked Tweedle-Z again to ask me where we were.

It was some random road in the middle of nowhere. I had no idea. I recalled my confession statement when I had told them that on the day of the invasion we had pulled back some kilometres from our original position near Pavlopil. They brought me a map and I started looking for landmarks that I could remember. After some time dweedling about, we found out where that spot was, an abandoned cattle-feed station. They took some photos of me at the position for their investigation. What nailed it for me was the sight of some of our old vehicles that we had set fire to, to prevent the enemy from using them. Our company mechanics truck had been stripped by locals and dumped to the side of the road, but our battalion logo was still visible on the side. We went into the feed station and found the room where we'd slept that night. Russian soldiers had obviously moved in after our exit. You could see a pigsty of abandoned Russian ration packs littering the floor.

Once I was done confirming this was indeed one of the places where we had stayed, they gave me a cigarette. I stood around smoking with Kosovan, my so-called lawyer, and the guard who had changed my cuffs. We talked about this and that while Brahim was giving his statement to the investigators. After that, we got back into the vans and made our way to Pavlopil. The guard who was looking after me shared the packed lunch his wife had made for him. Her sausage rolls were superb. God, they tasted good. 'I wish my fiancée could cook like this,' I joked.

After a bit Tweedle-Z turned around and saw that I did not have my bag on my bonce, so he ordered the guard to put it over my head. Blindsided, I knew that we were approaching Pavlopil from the west and that we would come to a bridge which we had tried to blow up on our exit, to slow down the Russian advance. The bridge was still standing but was obviously damaged in some way. The van pulled up and the others discussed whether it would be safe to risk crossing it. 'It doesn't look safe,' someone said. I found this rather amusing but stayed shtum.

The van moved forward and eventually we stopped. They took the bag off my head and I looked around. We were at the entrance to Pavlopil and it brought back a lot of memories. I felt sad and pretty emotional to be back in the old place. It hadn't changed much, the war seemed to have missed it. They wanted to know where my company HQ was and we set off, walking, because it was not very far. The house we were based in had been spray-painted with massive 'Z's all over the place, but it was now abandoned and mother nature was coming back. Images of our guys messing about, laughing, telling great stories, flooded into mind and it felt sad, desperately so, to see so many 'Z's where we had been.

They photographed and filmed me again, pointing out evidence proving that I had been here for their investigation. Once we had finished that, they asked me where my position had been. We had been joined by some Russian soldiers who looked as though they knew what they were doing. I started to worry because we might end up in the mortar pit where I had hidden a grenade by a ton of mortars and I, with them, would then be hoist by my own petard. I told them that it was a fair old schlep on foot and they decided that they didn't have time to do it – and, I think, they didn't like the idea of wandering around a place that could well be booby-trapped.

How right they were.

They asked me where the battalion HQ was and I pointed up the road from us. We set off on foot and I walked past some of the locals I recognized from the four years I had lived in the village. They didn't react to me or me to them, but I could only imagine what they felt, seeing me being marched past in handcuffs, escorted by a dozen officials and guards. At the HQ, more photos and videos were taken.

Tweedle-Z asked a stupid question: 'Do you know if anyone raped or harmed the civilians here?' I wanted to reply, 'I served in the Ukrainian, not the Russian army', but once again I held my tongue.

The local shops were just up the road from us, and I was a little nervous that we might end up going there. Someone asked one of the investigators if they wanted an ice cream. They had some 99s or whatever, but no ice cream for me. We drove over to the shops but only one of them was open. The second, closed shop had been my favourite. It was owned by a sweet elderly lady who had lived in Pavlopil her whole life. Her husband had been killed by the separatists and she was hardcore pro-Ukrainian, once telling me off for speaking Russian. I can only hope that she and her daughter got away before the Russians arrived.

The other shop was working but I didn't want to go in. I knew the shopkeeper and she knew me, but I didn't want to jeopardize her safety. We got back into the van and returned to the company HQ while Shaun and Brahim strutted their stuff for the investigation. When they were done, we headed off to Mariupol. When I was bagged up I tilted my head so that I could peek out of my left eye.

Christ! The road into Mariupol was grim, far grimmer than I imagined it would be. The sides of the road were littered with wrecked vehicles and bombed-out buildings: not a window or wall or roof was intact. The whole place had been pulverized. We arrived at the Illich steelworks, but when my bag was taken off I didn't recognize it. The old place had been hit by an apocalypse: buildings flattened, brick walls tumbled, machinery blackened, roofs holed, everything that could burn burnt. They faffed around for a bit, waiting for someone, and Tweedle-Z said, 'Aslin, do you want to meet the Chechens?'

'No.' My heart was palpitating.

He laughed: yet another joke but not a funny one. He was talking about the Kadyrovites, the pro-Chechen fighters who had a terrible reputation, even amongst the Russian army. We drove on to the main gates of the steelworks and out of the window I saw two Chechens with huge beards wearing the same military get-up popular with jihadi Muslim fighters: no body armour, just chest rigs because, if they are going to die, then God has willed it. As we drove past the Chechens, one of the Russians in the van joked: 'Akhmat Sila!' – referring to Kadyrov's old man who was not strong but dead, blown up in the bomb explosion at the Victory Parade in Grozny back in 2004. The joke was sarcastic, and I sensed some of the tension between the Russians and the Chechens.

The steelworks looked like a movie set for Stalingrad. It had been shredded, in a far worse state than the day I had surrendered. As we approached one of the buildings I saw a group of roughly fifty Chechens in full kit. I was praying that we wouldn't have any interaction with them because I doubted the ability of my hosts to protect me from them. The thing I was really scared of was for one of the investigators to tell the Chechens that I had fought with the Kurds in Syria. From the look of them, I would not have been at all surprised if there were a few former Islamic State fighters amongst them.

The day was getting long and the investigators were becoming frustrated with my inability to locate our battalion bunker. We got out of the car and then they tried to figure out which way to go. They kept asking me if I recognized this area. I told them no. Our battalion bunker was further north inside the steelworks. I showed them where it was on the map and that we had to drive there. They weren't up for that so they made me do the video and the photos talking about the battalion bunker in the wrong place. Their investigation was a bit rubbish, frankly, but remember the whole thing rested on extreme violence. Had I not been tortured, stabbed and listened to the sound of a man being clubbed to death, I would not have been cooperating with them.

Just as we finished, Tweedle-Z pointed to a curiosity. It was one of those tourist signposts that shows distances to other countries' cities. London was some 2,702.77 kilometres away. It felt further.

'Home?' Tweedle-Z joked.

Bastard.

As we were getting ready to move to the next location, the Azov base in the Azovstal steelworks, I was no longer needed because, unlike Shaun and Brahim, I hadn't been there. Brahim's translator was a distinguished old gentle-man who spoke English and French, and he was far nicer and smarter than my female translator with the awful pong perfume. He explained that I would no longer be required, but that some Russians wanted to speak to me. Once again, panic and dread consumed me.

A brand-new silver Mercedes pulled up and then I was bagged so competently that I couldn't see where we were going or who were my new captors. The Merc sashayed through the rubble, driving fast, God knows where. After a time I heard the distinctive clanking of the SIZO prison gates opening, so we were back to 'Go'. I was debagged, hooded and returned to my cell for just five minutes before I was called out again.

'Aslin!'

'*Slava Rossiya! Slava Rossiya! Slava Rossiya! Akhmat Sila! Donbas Sila!*' I knew the drill. Hooded once more, arms in the black dolphin position, I was walked to the courtyard where they removed the hood and I was placed in the cage in the back of a police van, very much like the ones they have in Britain. As I was clambering on board, I noted that the van's plates were not from Donetsk but were Russian.

Oh, fuck.

I began to fear they might be taking me to the black site where they were holding Shaun and Brahim. It was anx-iety attack time. As my fears consumed me, it was truly awful, but there was nothing I could do except wait and see. I tried to peek through the gaps in the cage at the top towards the front. We were driving through the centre of Donetsk until the van slowed and turned into a small alley.

A gate opened and we drove into a courtyard. The building was rather grand – the most upmarket place I had been in so far – and someone came to the back of the van, unlocked the cage and let me out. He was in his early fifties, well-built, and clearly looked after himself well.

'Aslin, hold your hands out,' he said in fluent English, placing some really fancy black handcuffs on me. He was wearing a high-spec Russian army uniform and looked cool, unlike Tweedle-Z or Knifeman or all the rest of the DPR – Ukrainian traitors – I had had the misfortune to come across. He also looked as though he could kill me in two seconds, if he chose to.

He led me up the steps into the main reception area and through a maze of hallways and corridors, the only sound our steps. The building seemed empty. In some of the rooms we passed I saw glimpses of Russian kitbags but no people. When we came to our destination, the door was locked. He tried to open the door but after a beat he kicked it open. Not a good sign. I thought, right, they are going to beat the shit out of me, all over again, but this time this guy is seriously good at this stuff.

He sat me down on a chair, then pulled up another chair and sat in front of me and explained that he was from the Investigative Committee of the Russian Federation – Следственный комитет Российской Федерации. I noticed his epaulette had three stars set in a triangle formulation, so he was a colonel. In simple terms, he was the heavy mob. There were two criminal cases against me for being a mercenary, he said, one in the DPR and one in the Russian Federation. We had to wait a little, he said, for a translator and my lawyer to arrive. He asked me if I was hungry or needed something to drink. Fearing being beaten, I declined the offer of food but asked for a drink. A guard turned up while the colonel wandered off somewhere else, to kick doors down or whatnot.

I looked round the room; you could see marks on the wall where posters and other stuff had been before they were removed by the occupiers. This had been a Ukrainian office building before the new 'owners' had moved in. As with UBOP, EVS and SIZO, I tried to remember key details which would help me geo-locate this place, if I ever got out of here. But it was tricky because we were over-looked by other high-rise buildings. From the sound of traffic and the density of the high-rises, the best I could do was place us in the dead centre of Donetsk.

The colonel came back with a bottle of water, followed by a new figure who was introduced to me as my second lawyer, the one for my Russian case. An older man with a grey beard and a goatee, he wore a cheap and cheesy suit and turned out to be as useless as Lawyer Number One. The blonde translator with the awful pong perfume rocked up and we began.

The colonel sat behind his desk and got his laptop out of his bag and a portable printer. He explained to me that he could go over the whole case from the get-go or base much of it on the testimony I had already given to the DPR investigation. Like so many others locked inside a criminal justice system I had no faith in, I just wanted them to get on with it. So, I accepted that the Russian case against me would ride alongside the DPR one.

Even so, the colonel had a ton of questions for me, where had I been, had I worked with or for the British and the Americans, et cetera. One question both scared and intrigued me: 'Were you serving with the Ukrainian army? If so, have you the paperwork to prove it?'

I replied that I had joined up in 2018 at the military recruitment office and then that I had undergone military training in Mykolaiv, that I had my military ID card. He told me that wouldn't work. He needed my enlistment contract with the Ukrainian Ministry of Defence. The truth was that I didn't have it on me, but Diana had it when she fled Ukraine. I could get hold of it if they would allow me to make one phone call, but I was afraid to go there. I didn't trust him, I didn't trust the system here, I didn't trust any of it. So absolute was my distrust that I didn't supply the thing that might have saved me.

Perhaps.

Lawyer Number Two was no good either. Most of the time he was just another interrogator, throwing me hostile questions that a defence lawyer should be challenging, not introducing. But the colonel's game was different, very well organized, even down to the way he laid his stuff out on the desk in a certain order. He gave off the vibe of a proper military man and seemed relaxed enough for me to ask a big question.

'What will happen if the Russian Federation decide to charge me?'

'Personally, I think you will be exchanged before that happens.' A glimmer of hope flickered inside me. It was the first time I had heard something positive. But was this another trick? He finished up and said we would probably be seeing each other a few more times. He packed his stuff up and then took me back outside to the minivan. I got in and away we went again, but we made a stop at a kebab shop. While the others tucked in, I regretted saying I wasn't hungry. The colonel asked me if I was still thirsty and I said yes, so he gave me a litre bottle of fizzy water which I necked sharpish.

And then it was back to SIZO. The colonel's words, that I would probably be traded before the event of a Russian trial, were a source of hope, but my optimism was crushed by the reality of being hooded and frogmarched through SIZO by Three Four. I had to contend with the immediate moronic brutality in my face; that the future might be better – that I even had a future – seemed absurd. At night, there were times when my gloom seemed to overwhelm me.

Six o'clock: rise and shine, sing the fucking Russian anthem, then: 'Aslin!'

'*Slava Rossiya! Slava Rossiya! Slava Rossiya! Akhmat Sila! Donbas Sila!*'

Hood on, handcuffs on, do the black dolphin, on repeat. Back in the paddy wagon, off to court, then into a cell, then from there back into the paddy wagon because they had taken me to the wrong entrance, then into a different entrance, a new cell, then I heard Shaun and Brahim outside, then into a big cage along one wall of the court. They took off my handcuffs and in I went.

Show time.

Two cameras, one for the court, one for the dock, a dais

for the judges, two tables, one for the prosecutors, one for the defence, at the back a crowd of Russian journalists. A few moments later Shaun and Brahim came in. We had a quiet natter. I told them that my family were raising merry hell through the Foreign Office. And that the goons had killed a fellow prisoner in SIZO. Shaun said that they had been moved from the black site to the Makiivka Pretrial Prison where conditions were a lot better. Our translators trooped in, my lady with her awful pong perfume, Brahim's civilized gent, and Shaun had an older lady with dyed black hair. Next, the lawyers rocked up. We had not been able to talk to them because real justice was not the point of the shadow game that was about to be staged.

They had decided because of the seriousness of the charges, some of which carried the death sentence, that they would try the case with not one but three judges. For some reason they asked our permission for this move, and we agreed. When the trial got going, it was hard to follow the translator, and hard to keep up with all the jargon and all the subclauses. It was mercenary this and mercenary that, and that conspiracy, blah blah blah.

I was the first of the three of us called to speak. I told them how I came to fight for the Ukrainian army, how I ended up in the Donbas. Sometimes a judge or a prosecutor would ask a question, but I was confused and didn't understand the rules of the game. In particular, I didn't understand the consequences of what I was admitting to. Then they played with Shaun, then Brahim.

During Brahim's evidence, Shaun and I discussed the

charge of being a mercenary. As we had been told, this was the big one, the one that the DPR media and radio were always going on about, the one that carried the death sentence. The three of us decided that we would plead guilty to all the other, lesser charges, but go with 'not guilty' on being a mercenary. Our logic was simple: one, we were not mercenaries and we could prove it, if allowed; two, this charge was the one that could end with us being executed.

The senior judge asked me to stand.

'Aiden Daniel John Mark Aslin' – why I have so many middle names is beyond me – 'Do you plead guilty to terrorist weapons training?'

'Yes, sir.'

'Do you plead guilty to the forcible seizure of power or the forcible retention of power?'

'Yes, sir.'

'Do you plead guilty to being a mercenary?'

'No, sir.' A hush fell on the court. The stupefied look on my lawyer's face told the story. My translator asked me if I was sure.

'Yes, not guilty on the mercenary part.'

Shaun and Brahim followed suit, pleading guilty to all the nonsense but not guilty to the big one, of being a mercenary. As they went through the hoops, my lawyer was gesturing to me, why did you say that? The pressure grew and I asked the translator if we could speak to our lawyers. Permission was granted and the court went into recess.

My lawyer came over to me: 'What are you doing?'

'Listen, we are recognized as servicemen and this charge carries the death sentence. We are not mercenaries under international law.'

'International law does not exist here.' That hit me in the gut but what he said next really floored me: 'The mercenary charge carries a sentence of only seven years. You should change your plea to guilty because, if not, it will make it more difficult later when we appeal the death sentence.'

'What death sentence?'

'You have pleaded guilty to forcible seizure of power or the forcible retention of power. Under Article 323 of the Criminal Code of the DPR, that carries the death sentence.'

We had been conned. I felt like someone who had bought a rubbish timeshare in Tenerife, but that was about losing money. This low, dirty trick meant we could lose our lives. Throughout the pressure, the state propaganda, all the talk from the lawyers and prosecutors and interrogators was that we were mercenaries and that carried the death sentence. That is what Graham Phillips had said. And all of that was a lie. The big one was not being a mercenary. The big one was overthrowing the DPR. And we had all pleaded guilty to that. Our defence lawyers were party to the con. At no time had they explained the consequences of Article 323 to us clearly, in plain Russian. We were not fools. We had been deliberately deceived. Trapped as we were, it now made sense to plead guilty to the lesser charge of being a mercenary so that we might not be handed a death sentence.

The judges came back, heard our revised guilty pleas on the mercenary charges, and decided to deliberate on the sentencing and return in the morning. The lawyers and the translators left, leaving the three of us in our cage, stunned.

The guards came for Shaun and Brahim first. The guard who was escorting me had to wait for one of the others to come back. The court had emptied, so there was just him and me, waiting in the cage. He saw that I was broken.

'Johnny,' his voice was so quiet it was almost on the edge of hearing, 'all this is bullshit. Blah blah blah. It's Hollywood. When it's finished, you will go home.'

The other guard appeared and he fell silent. Back in the paddy wagon, back to the cell. My cellmates thought talk of a death sentence was a scare tactic, that they would never go through with it.

The judges let us stew, compounding my dread. But I was not left alone.

'Aslin! Lie down!'

'Yes, sir!'

'Aslin, stand up!'

'*Slava Rossiya! Slava Rossiya! Slava Rossiya! Akhmat Sila! Donbas Sila!*'

This time they took me to the propaganda studio room. The MGB goons Popov and Vlad worked me hard, making me put in a series of calls to the Foreign Office, Parliament, Number 10, begging for the British government to make contact with the DPR to organize our exchange. For some unknown reason, they had dropped the stuff about exchanging with Medvedchuk. The new big thing was for Britain to engage with the DPR, which would mean they could crow that they had been officially recognized. I could have been a contender for an Oscar, such was the fear and trepidation I put in my voice. The fear was real, but I also knew that the more I pleased the MGB, the more likely the possibility that they would put in a good word for us.

It's also fair to say that I had built up a reasonable relationship with both Popov and Vlad, that they had come to treat me decently because it was clear I was willing to work hard for what they wanted to achieve. The payback for me was getting calls through to Mum during which she would fill me in with what the Foreign Office were up to and news such as her planned meeting with the Ukrainian ambassador to London. It meant a lot, knowing that Shaun, Brahim and I had not been forgotten.

Every once in a while, I would hit Popov with an innocent, indirect question: 'I'm so scared, I just hope I can see my family.'

'You just need to be patient,' he said. That felt like he agreed with the courthouse guard, that the trial was just Hollywood, blah, blah, blah. I hoped that was right, while in the confines of my cell I fought off my demons.

Six o'clock in the morning. God, how I hated singing that fucking anthem.

'Aslin!' Russia is great, et cetera, et cetera, the usual, black dolphin, hooded, cuffed, paddy wagon. One of the escort guards was an old chap and gentle with it and he asked me, kindly, how I was feeling. Everyone knew about what was happening to us because it was the lead story on the DPR news.

'Scared,' I said.

'There's a moratorium on the death sentence,' the guard told me. 'This means that even if you are sentenced to death there is no legal mechanism in place to carry it out.'

Still, my mouth went dry. I was hooded but I heard the guards chat about how many journalists there were outside the court precinct, waiting to get a photo of us. I had become a Donetsk People's Republic local celebrity. Down some steps into a holding tank, on my tod, then Shaun and Brahim rocked up, up the stairs into the corridor, just shy of the entrance to the court cage. Even from the corridor we could hear a lot of chatter from the court. Faced with a lot of attention, the guards got tough and mine locked me in the classic rough-handle pose, head in my knees, arms behind my back.

The courtroom was packed with Russian journalists, in for the kill. Everyone filed in, the judges last, and the boss judge read out our sentences, mine first. Maybe it was alphabetical. His voice was as dry as dust, the legal she-nanigans hard to follow, but when he got to Article 323 of the Criminal Code of the DPR, I was all ears.

'Having committed actions against the constitutional order of the Donetsk People's Republic, and attempting to overthrow the government, it is justified and objective to hand down the highest possible punishment: the death sentence.'

Fuck.

My heart thumped. I had no words. The thing I had dreaded since Graham Phillips first pushed it down my throat, the possibility of being executed for simply being a Ukrainian soldier fighting Russian fascism, was now a fact.

Brahim and Shaun got the same. Pleading guilty to being a mercenary hadn't worked. Doing all their wretched propaganda videos hadn't worked. All of the sweet talk from the Russian colonel, the courtroom guard and the old guard in the paddy wagon: none of it had worked. We were going to be executed. I wanted to cry but, somehow, I couldn't.

The judges and our hopeless lawyers retired and the press pack moved right up to our cage as fast and as likeable as the velociraptors in *Jurassic Park*.

They wanted a quote. I delivered a line given to me by the MGB goons the day before, in this eventuality: 'I was hoping the sentence would be a lot fairer, judging the circumstances in which I helped the investigation and also because I surrendered to the Donetsk People's Republic. I wish it could be different, but God will be the one that will judge me when the time comes.'

The stuff about God was my idea. Listen, I'm no Holy Joe, but I thought that a bit of God might convey that I wasn't a mindless killer, that people in Britain and the wider world might understand that there was something wrong about the trial. Shaun looked pretty grim. Of the three of us, Brahim did best, smiling, trolling the whole dark nonsense.

'Hi, Mum! Happy days!' Brahim said. Part of me was worried that he was asking to get the shit kicked out of him the moment we went down; part of me thought that he was Lorenzo the Fucking Magnificent.

Then we were taken down. The guard who had told me the trial was all Hollywood was my escort. When we were on our own, I asked him: 'Boss, can I have a fag?'

'Yes, one moment.' The gift of a cigarette from a guard at that moment was something beautiful, but it did not puncture my deep, oceanic gloom. I sat on my own in the court's holding tank, staring at the floor, hearing the words of the judge proclaiming the death sentence over and over again.

When I got to the paddy wagon, the guard who normally looked after me hadn't heard the news: 'What did you get?'

'Death.'

'Nah, they're not going to do it. There's a ban on it. They have sentenced seven people to death in Donetsk and they are all still very much alive.'

These kind words, too, failed to shake the utter blackness of my despair. The beating, the stabbing, the killing of a fellow prisoner, the relentless propaganda I had been used for had shredded my spirit. I was a fucking mess and I couldn't deal with this, the hardest blow of all.

Back in my cell, the guys had saved me lunch. The generosity of the wretched is a wonderful thing. I washed my face with some cold water.

'So?' Vova asked.

'Death.'

I sat down on the small stool processing everything that had happened. I started to swing my upper body back and forth to try to get some comfort, my right leg ticking up and down, uncontrollably. My leg still does this to this day. Maybe it's restless legs syndrome. The doctor says it's anxiety.

Later that evening we heard on the DPR radio that Shaun, Brahim and I had been sentenced to death. It was official.

Again, that feeling of emptiness.

## Chapter Fourteen

# Bad Wolf

The MGB goons left me in my cell for a long time, a cruel and clever trick played on my family, leaving them in the dark as to my fate, and a cruel and clever trick against me, too. It's hard to get across just how bleak my mood was during that time. Whenever I tried to put myself back together again, a fresh burst of propaganda would come over the radio on the prison Tannoy, hammering down the fact that the two British 'mercenaries' had been sentenced to death and, yet again, I would be consumed by a great wave of anxiety.

Eventually, after two and a half weeks of agony, I heard the guards in the hallway come to our door. We all shot up, ready to lie down.

'Aslin! Lie down!'

'Yes, sir!'

'Aslin! Stand up!'

'*Slava Rossiya! Slava Rossiya! Slava Rossiya! Akhmat Sila! Donbas Sila!*'

Hooded and cuffed, I did the black dolphin out of our

cell block and towards the gates, but then we turned off towards the propaganda room. The hood was removed and Popov and Vlad sat behind the desk.

'Hi,' Popov said. 'So it's been some time since we last met. How do you feel about the sentence?'

'Scared. I don't know what's going to happen.'

They told me they were going to call the Foreign Office and they wanted me to ask them what the Ukrainian ambassador had told my mother. I had a nice chat – in the circumstances – with the duty clerk. He asked me if I had heard from Shaun and Brahim. I told him that they were fine, which was a lie because I had not seen them since the sentencing. What did the Ukrainian ambassador say to my mum? I asked. The Foreign Office clerk was not born yesterday and gave nothing away – knowing that others would be listening in – but said that measures were being taken to ensure our release.

He finished off in a really lovely way: 'Aiden, you are protected under international law by the Geneva Convention.'

'I'm scared,' I replied. 'That's bullshit. Nothing is being done.'

That last bit was for the goons. It was great for the goons to hear the line about the Geneva Convention and when I returned to the cell I was in a better mood.

One Sunday at around nine o'clock in the evening we were startled by the sudden appearance of Three Four opening the peephole and telling me to collect my stuff and leave the cell. This made me extremely anxious because movement on Sundays never happened. I said goodbye to my great Ukrainian cellmates – I would really miss them – and some of them wondered whether I was going to be exchanged. Once again, this is hard to describe, but all of us together had listened to someone being beaten to death in the next cell. We had been through so much. These guys, to me, were brothers. They checked that I knew all their surnames properly so that, if I was being traded, I could get in touch with their families and say that their boys were alive once I was back in Blighty.

Three Four was back at the door.

'*Slava Rossiya! Slava Rossiya! Slava Rossiya! Akhmat Sila! Donbas Sila!*'

Then we hit the deck. They called my name and I nodded to the lads and left that cell for the last time. Although cuffed and hooded, I knew the geography of the prison blindfolded by now. The exit out of the cell block was to the left. We turned right. The moment we did so, my hopes were crushed. I wasn't going home.

They took me to an empty cell, decorated with unwelcoming graffiti: 'Death to Ukrainians!' and 'Death is your only way out' in Russian. The isolation deepened my fear. Suddenly I heard the door being unlocked, so I chanted '*Slava Rossiya!*' and dropped to the floor, turning my head so that I could sneak a look at who might be joining me.

It appeared to be Ben Gunn, his beard and hair so matted and filthy to make him look like the marooned pirate from *Treasure Island*. The guard ordered me to explain the prison rules to the new guy and as I was doing so, he smiled.

'I know the rules, Johnny.'

It was Vjekoslav Prebeg, a Croatian in our marine battalion and a good friend. I had not seen him since I had surrendered and we quickly caught up on all the gossip over a dinner of gruel with extra lumps in it. The guard returned with a razor and some blades and ordered me to hack off my new cellmate's beard and matted locks. As I did so, he told me his story.

Prebeg, as I called him, had got out of the steelworks on the night of April 11th, walking through thick fog, out of the city. On the second day his group was spotted and came under artillery fire. Some people surrendered, but Prebeg managed to stick with a smaller group of around seventeen who carried on, heading north, to Ukrainian lines 140 kilometres away. They got pretty close after nine days of walking but were captured by the enemy within spitting distance of the front line. And then the bad stuff happened.

'First, they hit me on the nose, breaking it. Then the questions began. You have three seconds to come up with something. If you don't answer, they hit you again. They hit me on the body, the head, the face. I was lucky, none of my teeth were knocked out. They used builder's pipes made of heavy-duty plastic to hit me. And electric shocks from a field phone. I tried not to scream but you can't help it. They would connect the clips to my skin around the kidney and my fingers, and the current would make my body arc in agony. It was dark. Then they played around with a gun, putting a bullet in the chamber and holding it at my head.'

I told him that I had been beaten and stabbed and sentenced to death and that a prisoner, probably a guy from the Azov Battalion, had been beaten to death in a next-door cell. Prebeg had grim news about a British civilian aid worker, Paul Urey, who had been captured by the

Russians. Prebeg had seen him at the prosecutors' office a few days previously and he was in a bad way, throwing up, the guards refusing to give him water. Since then, Prebeg had heard that poor Paul Urey had died.

With Prebeg's beard trimmed and hair cut – to be honest, I did a terrible job – the guard collected the razor and blades and we fell asleep.

Six o'clock, we were woken by the prison Tannoy, and then, half-asleep, we sang the fucking Russian anthem. Still, Prebeg was funny and kind and sympathetic, and talking through everything made that hateful place less grim.

Prebeg had faced the same nonsense about being accused of being a mercenary as I had, but he had made a mistake. He had kept his phone on him and not deleted anything, so that when he was caught by surprise, they got his phone too. Under torture he revealed the password and so they were able to download everything. This scared me because I had sent Prebeg a message after our mortar unit had hit a Russian target and our intelligence confirmed that we had killed a Russian soldier. If the Russians or their proxies found that, I would be in even bigger trouble than I already was – although it's hard to think what's worse than being on Death Row. However, Prebeg dampened my fears when he explained that they found his contract with the Ukrainian Ministry of Defence. The Russian colonel I had met noted the contract, proving he was not a mercenary, and had changed his status in the Russian case from accused to witness.

'What effect will that have on the DPR prosecution against me?' Prebeg had asked the colonel.

'That depends on which case Moscow wants to go with' – that struck us as proof that the whole DPR trial, indeed, the whole thing, was a Kremlin sock puppet. We didn't know how the trials would pan out. Still, we had time enough to work through the possibilities. In fact, all the time in the world.

One evening, around seven o'clock, Three Four was having fun getting everyone to shout rubbish. He would yell: 'Zelenskiy!'

And we would have to shout: 'Pederast!'

He would shout: 'Putin!'

And we would have to shout: 'President of the world!'

I had completely switched off, running on autopilot, my mind wandering into my inner subconscious. So, when Three Four shouted 'Putin!' I shouted back 'Khuylo!' – 'dickhead' in Russian.

I instantly froze at the sudden realization of what I had just yelled. Prebeg turned to me and asked, with real dread in his voice, 'What did you just *do*?'

Staring at the wall, I hunted in my mind for something to explain my ocean-going foolishness. It was like that scene in *Ghostbusters* when Ray accidentally thinks of the Stay Puft Marshmallow Man – and something truly bad is going to happen. We had good reason to be scared because Three Four was the most sadistic guard of them all, by a country mile. We stood, rigid with fear, waiting for them to come. Three Four would love nothing better than to beat us for any small thing – let alone calling Putin a dickhead.

'Who was that?' asked Three Four.

'Johnny,' replied 'Pops', one of the older guards and not a bad guy.

'Seriously?' said Three Four. And then he started to laugh.

Still we stood, unmoving, the tension in my neck unbearable. That night was grim, we were on edge for hour after hour. When they yelled at us to go to sleep, I lay in my bed, fearing that they would come in the middle of the night, the better to teach me the harshest kind of lesson. It took a long time to work it out. After poor Paul Urey had died, the guards had been given a real bollocking for not keeping him alive – the Kremlin and its proxies are more afraid of bad publicity than they pretend – and they were under strict instructions not to harm the foreign prisoners. So we were, in a funny sort of way, in protective custody – and that meant I got away with shouting out that Putin was a dickhead in one of the worst places on earth to do such a thing.

One day the guard rocked up, I did the Slava chant, hit the floor, stood up, was cuffed and hooded and taken to the propaganda suite, but just before we got there the guard removed the hood. This had never happened to me before. In the room were Popov and Vlad and a third man, John Mark Dougan. He was an American oddball who, very much like Graham Phillips, had started a new career as a Kremlin propaganda monkey. He blinked all the time, which I've read might be a form of Tourette's, where your body's twitches may suggest some underlying psychological problem. Dougan had been a US Marine, then a cop with the Palm Beach Police Department. But he fell out badly with his bosses and after escaping the FBI's clutches he ended up in Russia. He had claimed that another cop had given him, before he died, a copy of secret sex kompromat tapes of the rich and famous made by Jeffrey Epstein, the multimillionaire paedophile, friend of Prince Andrew, Duke of York, and Ghislaine Maxwell, daughter of tycoon Robert Maxwell. Dougan said that he had not shared the tapes with the Russians. Yeah, right.

By this stage my shoes had fallen apart and he brought me some new ones, but Dougan's gift came with a little poison all of its own. He told me that RT, the Russian propaganda channel, were going to film our interview in a few minutes but he wanted to sort some stuff out beforehand. He said that he had powerful friends in Moscow who could help me. The death sentence could be dropped, but in return they would like a favour, that I, with my background fighting in Syria, would say on camera that Ukraine had been covertly selling the NLAWs and Javelin missiles provided by the British and Americans to the Kurdish Peshmerga – for big money. Dougan wasn't making this claim himself, but obviously my statement would cause two bits of trouble the Kremlin would relish: the first bit, between the British and the Americans and the Ukrainians; the second bit, between the Ukrainians and the Turkish government, who were no fans of arming the Kurds. I was uneasy because this claim was wholly untrue and that could sour things with the British Foreign Office, who were my great hope of getting us out of jail. That said, I was their plaything, their bitch, and I feared that if I didn't play along, things would go badly for me.

Dougan clinched it when he pointed to another stranger

in the room, a civilian in tactical clothing, and said: 'He's FSB. Look, he's even got his gun on him.' Good observation. By this point I knew that not even the MGB goons were allowed to bring their guns into prison. Even the Russian colonel handed his in. So the guy with Dougan had to be big potatoes: FSB.

So, I am ashamed to say, I did it. I hoped that my friends and the people in the British Foreign Office would work out that what I was saying was nonsense. But then I came up with a wheeze to ram that message home. Towards the end of the video, I asked permission to sing the Russian national anthem and Dougan, fool that he is, fell for it. So, you have me on video belting out that fucking song. Point being, it was bleeding obvious that someone would have had to hit me very hard a lot of times before I learnt the Russian anthem nigh-on word-perfect. So, for once, I felt as though I'd fucked Dougan and his pal in the FSB and the whole sorry shower of them.

My take on Dougan was that there was something wrong with him. Like Phillips, he had some weird personality disorder that made him see the world upside down and wrong way round. There's a ton of things wrong with the United Kingdom and the United States of America, but to get into bed with Vladimir Putin's Russia – a regime whose soldiers rape, castrate and torture – that is sick. Sure, Dougan was less of a scumbag than Phillips. But in my book, which this is, he's still a scumbag.

## CHAPTER FIFTEEN

# Knights in Dark Satin

Three Four was a toad squatting on my soul. As the days dragged on, and no word came of what was going to happen to us – to be traded or to be executed – I feared that I would crack up completely. Sadist though he was, Three Four could somehow smell my anxiety about my fate.

'Aslin, why haven't you been shot yet?' He cracked that joke about once a day.

As summer drew on, all the windows in SIZO were thrown open. The consequence is that every time they forced some poor devil to run the gauntlet or used a taser against a helpless Ukrainian prisoner of war, we could hear the screams, twice over. Once when they happened and once again in the small hours of the night when your imagination recreated them. I still had flashbacks of the time they clubbed to death the poor man in the next-door cell. The feeling of gloom deepened when in late July we heard on the DPR radio that the Ukrainians had used their artillery to blow up a prisoner-of-war camp at Olenivka near Donetsk, killing fifty-three of their own people.

The clock just struck thirteen.

In my experience, the Ukrainian army was extremely wary of using artillery without seriously good intelligence because supplies were so constrained and that was the way our army was run. Why on earth would the Ukrainians want to kill more than fifty of their own people? The majority of them were from the Azov Battalion. The alternative possibility was that the Russians bombed their own prison, to cover up the fact that they had tortured and maybe even killed a good number of the Azov people already. Later on, I met a fellow who had been in Olenivka and survived the explosion.

'I heard no artillery,' he told me.

If the Russians could kill fifty-three prisoners of war and then lie about it, then what chance they would show some mercy to us three?

Since being taken captive, I hadn't been able to cry once. Even after being condemned to death, no tears would flow. I had wanted to cry but I was running on empty. Somehow, there was no fuel to actually process the death sentence. I desperately wanted to release the dark emotions swirling around inside me, but I couldn't do it. The only way I could cope with the stress of my anxiety attacks was to rock back and forth. The rocking gave me some comfort as I let my mind wander to a blank void, away from this small dark cell.

A few months earlier I remember chatting with Yaroslav, one of my friends in my first cell in SIZO. He was a young soldier with an appetite to learn English and I taught him some new phrases. As we got closer, it became obvious that he trusted me, and during one of our discussions he told me he was so scared his fear was eating into him, and that he was thinking about cutting his wrists as a way out of this hellhole.

'Suicide is the only freedom the Russians can't take from us.'

I reached into the black pit where I keep my sense of humour and brought out a dark joke. He laughed, a little, and I did my best to try to reassure him and tell him everything would be OK: 'You're a soldier. This can't go on for ever. You will be exchanged.'

Two months on, it was my turn to struggle with living inside the dark and hateful box we were all trapped in. Prebeg and I found a razor hidden in the bars by the open window and decided to keep it. I had become sickened by my lack of courage. They had broken me, utterly, and the sole purpose of my existence was to quack their evil propaganda nonsense and sing the Russian anthem like a performing monkey. Humiliated, broken, cracking up, bullied by Three Four, my sense of self-worth was at rock bottom and I thought hard about killing myself. I longed to end it all. I spent a few nights unable to sleep, just thinking of taking the razor and using it on my wrists. I would bleed out and lie on my bed waiting for death and they would not even notice until morning. Inside my head I had constant arguments with myself between reason and dread. On top of everything else, I did not want to be shot. I would rather be hanged.

Living in a tiny box with one other person, you can't hide something as profound as suicidal depression. Prebeg caught my mood and gave me a verbal slap. He was hand-ling prison far better than I and so got to sleep a lot more quickly than I did. He would be snoozing away in the middle of the night when the temptation to slash my wrists was at its highest. I was convinced I could bear the pain and hide any sound.

So what stopped me? Prebeg. Not his actual words, but I worried about what they would do to him if I did kill myself. That was too much guilt to carry with me into whatever awaits after death.

Time treacled by. The rubbish defence lawyers had told us that the outcome of our appeal would be heard on Sep-tember 16th. That date came and went and still no news. September 23rd started like any other morning: the prison Tannoy clattering us awake, the singing of that fucking anthem, a rubbish breakfast, then shitting water because the prison food was so awful.

Prebeg and I were good friends, but occasionally we would have little tiffs where we would say, right, you stay on your side of the cell and I'll stick to my side. It was like living in a shoebox. We had no control as to what came over the prison Tannoy, and one awful psychological tor-ture was when they played Vladimir Solovyov's radio show. He is Putin's greatest apologist and how I fucking hate that man. The grim truth is that he is a clever and effective and intelligent broadcaster who spews out dark nonsense. Dyslexic, rubbish at school, self-taught, I wrestle with understanding how someone with natural intelligence can bring himself to work for the dark side. And Putin's regime is very dark indeed.

You had to listen hard to Solovyov to work out what was really happening in the world. It was like trying to solve a cryptic crossword. But from his vicious tirade, we worked out backwards that the Russians were losing ground in the Kharkiv oblast. That was cool.

Then all of a sudden Mr Khorosho's kindly voice could be heard talking to another guard, saying 'they are going home'.

Four words rang inside my head like a lightning flash.

Steps walking away. What the fuck was happening? Mr Khorosho was a good man and wouldn't have said that outside our cell with a malicious intent. But was it true? The thing that got to me, that I was afraid of, was not despair. Like John Cleese as the crazy time-obsessed guy in *Clockwise*, it's not the despair I was afraid of. It was the hope.

One hour later we heard something we had never heard before, a big group of Ukrainians in the courtyard chattering to each other. Prebeg and I talked it through, that most likely they were sending the Ukrainians to an official POW camp. They started singing the Russian national anthem. We knew that trick. Then we could hear the guards enter our cell block and unlock a cell not so far from ours. The prisoner's question was muffled, we could not make it out. But we heard the guard's reply: 'We are taking you to be shot!'

In prison, you learn to listen. In an evil prison, you learn to listen extraordinarily well.

'That's not right, something is going on,' I whispered to Prebeg. The guard's words were dark but, critically, the tone was not. There was a twinkle in his voice, a joke, not at the prisoner's expense, but, somehow, at the system.

The lunch trolley was late and we were starving. The door started to unlock so we did the chant, '*Slava Rossiya! Slava Rossiya! Slava Rossiya! Akhmat Sila! Donbas Sila!*', and dropped to the floor.

'Aslin!'

'Yes, boss!'

'Come here!'

I went to the door, spun round, my back facing them. They placed the hood on me and then I was moved to one side.

'Prebeg!'

'Yeah.'

'Come here!'

This was not normal. Hooded, we were walked out of our cell block. But would we go right to the propaganda room? Or straight on to the outside world?

We went straight on.

The guard removed our hoods and told me to follow him. I was so confused because he was so relaxed. I followed him around the corner and he took his phone out and pressed record.

'We've given you food, water, medical attention when needed. Is that correct?'

'Yes, sir.'

'While you've been here, you haven't been beaten? Is that correct?'

'Yes, sir.'

'Would you like to sing the Russian anthem?'

'Yes, sir.'

I started singing that dreadful song, amplified by the echo in the basement we were in. Another guard, at the back, said 'Fucking hell, that was beautiful.'

The guard who was videoing switched off record and said 'Good boy.'

The hardest thing for me to do was to contain my hope, in case this was yet another evil trick, like all the rubbish they had told me that being a mercenary carried the death sentence.

'Aiden, Aiden, stop presuming they are going to release you. You are going to regret it,' I told myself, again and again.

They put me in a small holding cell while I heard Prebeg being put through the same hoops. We heard the peephole in the door next to us open and suddenly we heard thirty voices sing out '*Slava Rossiya!*'

Then the guard asked, 'You are not going to pick up a weapon again, right?'

That question had my heart racing.

'Is this it? Is this it?' I whispered to Prebeg. 'Did he say what I think he just said?'

The guard opened our slit and we stood to attention. He asked, 'Who is this?'

'Prebeg and Aslin,' my pal replied.

'Ohhh Aslin, fuck me, you're fat.' Quite the compliment considering I had lost a lot of weight in captivity.

'Aslin, let's sing.'

I sang the fucking anthem, again. Then he let us stew some more. After a time, I heard another guard outside the cell ask what was happening.

'Обмен' – *Obmen* – in English: 'Exchange.'

'Did you hear that?' I whispered.

Prebeg remained quiet. He, too, was wrestling with the suspicion that this was yet another horrible trick. We were like dogs that had been beaten so often and so cruelly we cowered in the corner even when the door to our kennel was opened.

What followed was a tedious nightmare, of us hooded, the hoods sealed with duct tape, then thrown in the back of a crammed lorry for a long, painful journey that lasted hours, with no opportunities for a toilet break or to stretch our legs. One of us complained about the unbearable pain of not being able to move – and got tasered for his cheek.

Then out of the lorry. They took off the hoods. We could see that we were in Rostov-on-Don airport – in south-west Russia. I still was afraid.

The moment that it clicked for me was in the empty departure lounge – Russia has closed the airport for commercial flights because of its war next door – when I saw a bunch of geezers in dishdasha, the flowing white dresses Arab men wear, handing out water. Thirsty as hell, I swigged my bottle and then looked at the label: 'Bottled in Saudi Arabia'. Amongst them was a dude, hanging back, but somehow part of the show.

Russian military police, our new goons, loaded us on to the bus to the plane in an unusual way, forcing us to kneel down. The bus drove to the plane and stopped by a set of steps.

'You will go one by one,' a Russian military policeman said. 'You follow my exact instructions. Anyone who doesn't will be tasered.' This, it turned out, was the very last command from a Russian or their proxies to trouble us. I was first up the stairs, Shaun next.

The Saudis had sent a massive private jet, luxuriously kitted out. As I entered the cabin there was the dude standing by the door. I shook his hand and thanked him, but my emotions were so all over the place I had all but lost the ability to communicate.

'I'm glad that you are now safe,' said the dude to Shaun and me. 'Where are you from?' he asked.

'London,' Shaun replied, then asked, 'Where are you from?'

'London,' said the dude.

'You don't half look like Roman Abramovich,' said Shaun.

'I am Roman Abramovich,' he said.

Aha.

The doors to the plane closed and the great fancy jet throttled up and whooshed up into the air. We were out of that awful fucking place and on our way home.

As we were taking off, I smelt smoke. Tobacco smoke.

'Can you smell that?' I said to Shaun.

I gestured to one of the men in black, Saudi security, sitting opposite us, and asked if he had a cigarette. He didn't speak English but understood the gesture and pulled out a packet of fags. He handed one to Shaun and me and lit them. It was like being back in the sixties when airlines did not care about smoking on board planes.

It would be wrong to say we were treated like royalty. We were royalty. Once in the air, flight attendants came around with trays of posh sandwiches and kebabs. I hadn't eaten good food for half a year, more. It was fucking magic.

The Saudis gave us free iPhone 13s, a pack of clothes and a toilet bag. I went to the bathroom and threw away my lice-ridden prison clothes and gave myself a sponge bath to wash away months of prison filth. The smell of soap filled me with joy.

We did ask for alcohol and got a no. There is always something missing in paradise.

On landing in Riyadh, they smuggled us away from a mass of journalists to a vast banqueting hall, with trays loaded with gorgeous food. We met a Ukrainian official who shook our hands, and we did a photo shoot, then met some people from the British Embassy. Then the Saudi foreign minister, Prince Faisal bin Farhan Al Saud, rocked up and gave a short speech of welcome. Beaming down at us, not in person but from his portrait on the wall, was Crown Prince Mohammed bin Salman – also known as MBS, also known as Mr Bone Saw after the murder of the Saudi dissident Jamal Khashoggi back in October 2018. I am grateful to both Abramovich and MBS for fixing the trade. Shaun, Brahim and I were all traded along with some 200-plus Ukrainians, including the commander of the Azov Battalion and our boss, Bova, for fifty Russians and Medvedchuk. Putin the godfather had got his boy back.

But my gratitude to the Russian oligarch who served Vladimir Putin for a long time and, who knows, perhaps still does, and the Saudi prince who silences his critics, has its limits. To me, they are knights in dark satin, playing a game with the Kremlin for their own purposes.

And my friends and I, we were just the pawns.

We got an economy flight back to London and we were

hurried out of a back door to a hotel, where I met my brother, my sister, Mum and Diana. I explained what had happened: 'The bastards stabbed and beat the fuck out of me.'

It didn't matter now. Everything was going to be OK. I kissed Diana and, getting cocky, said: 'I told you I would come back.'

I was Putin's prisoner no more.

## CHAPTER SIXTEEN

# 'The Boy Who Lived'

Driving up the A1 with Diana, my mum, my sister at the wheel, I began to discover just an inkling of how awful it had been for my family and Diana, and yet how they had never, ever stopped fighting for me, of how brilliant they had all been. It all came in a rush, and then slowly I got the full picture.

Diana had a brutal time. The Russians came to the outskirts of our home town, Mykolaiv, and hit it hard with artillery. She spent most of the time in the bath because we don't have a basement. The bathroom had no windows, so she thought she would be safer there, and the bathtub itself gave her a little more protection.

'I was afraid,' she told us for this book. 'I was afraid all the time. The artillery never stopped. In the mornings I wasn't sure I would make it till night. At night I wasn't sure I would make it till the morning. I was afraid to do the washing because the sound of the washing machine reminded me of the sound of shelling. The nights were the worst. The street lights all over the city were off and we had been warned not to turn on our house lights because the Russians would bomb us if they saw lights. It was dark, darker than you can imagine. If you looked out of the window you couldn't see even the shapes of the trees. It was all just black. The shops were empty, no buses, no transport. I was a prisoner in our own home. When it was getting too bleak, I would sit on the inside of our front door and imagine the war was over and Aiden coming into the house with all his heavy bags like he always did.

'Our house was shaking because of the constant shelling. Some of the houses near by got hit. There was only one safe route left and by many happy coincidences I managed to get out. I took one bag with the important stuff and our cat, Jingles. Aiden had named him after the prisoner's mouse in the movie *The Green Mile*. I hated leaving our home. It felt like I was betraying Aiden. If he was still alive.

'I fled to Hungary. I had a terrible burden of guilt. Guilty for having food while he was starving, guilty for being safe while he was living under constant shelling, guilty for being warm and comfortable while he was living at the steelworks, guilty for being free while he was fight-ing for his life. The only thing that kept me sane was Jingles. Our cat was a complete pain in the ass but he was the reason I got up from bed in the mornings. No matter how broken I felt, I still had to get up to clean his shit and feed him. It was even funny to think that both Aiden and Jingles had spent the previous winter in the trenches of Donbas, but now Aiden was still in Donbas and Jingles was travelling the world, having nice food, a comfortable bed and cuddles, love and care. I'd never loved cats and was very angry when Aiden brought him home after deployment, but very soon he became family. He is very special and it became very important for me to save this cat. I thought if Jingles survives and will be fine, so Aiden would be fine, too.

'Messages from Aiden were more or less regular; he even managed to call me from time to time. He never complained, never got hysterical or panicked. He was making jokes; he promised he would come back. He sounded like he always does, he sounded like my Aiden. He was asking me to get a visa and go to the UK. I didn't want to but I also didn't want to argue with him. So I applied for a visa just to stop the argument. The next day after I applied for the visa, on April 12th, he got captured. That's when I decided a hundred per cent that I was going to the UK. I thought I could be more useful there.

'He managed to call me that morning. He was joking and telling me everything is gonna be fine. He said it's not gonna be a five-star hotel but at least he's gonna lose some weight. It sounded like it was me who was in such a shitty situation and he was trying to calm me down.

'There were two days of silence and on April 14th I saw the pictures and videos on the propaganda channels. I can't find words to describe what I felt. I would never wish anyone to feel anything like that. He was bruised, beaten, looked dehydrated and disoriented. He literally looked half-conscious and he was speaking Russian bullshit propaganda on the Russian federal broadcaster. How very convincing!

'After so many years the Russians still haven't learned how to make good propaganda. It was obvious he had been forced to talk like that. In one of the videos he called himself a mercenary. That's total bullshit. He would never call himself that. He hated when people called him a foreign volunteer. He would always say: "I'm not a volunteer, I'm a Ukrainian Marine, a Ukrainian Defender." Aiden was so proud to be a Ukrainian Marine. So I knew all of it was bullshit. He said what he had to say. I started getting a whole bunch of hate messages from strangers. They were calling me a Nazi, Aiden a mercenary, and describing in horrible detail what they would like to do to us. Some of my Facebook friends decided it was their moral duty to send me Aiden's pictures, of him beaten up, and the propaganda videos – as if I haven't seen all of that already. I had a phobia about social media, unknown numbers and mystery links. I was afraid one day I would see a video of the Russians torturing or even executing him. This made me, for a time, very sick and unstable in my mind. One of Aiden's friends, who was worried as much as we all were, said that the Russians had given Aiden to the Chechens and he was now in Chechnya in some basement where they were torturing him very cruelly, and that there were some videos of that. It wasn't true but it added to my woes.

'The visa came through. My friend Viktoriia and I drove from Hungary to Calais but when we got to England, they told me the cat can't enter the country. They held us for hours. After too long, I broke down in floods of tears, crying out that my boyfriend is being tortured by the Russians and you won't let his cat in, and the immigration people said, "OK, the cat can come in."

'So Jingles is now a British citizen.

'One day Aiden was allowed to make a video call for the first time. He looked a bit better than in previous pictures, they were trying to cover up his scar. But I could see he was alive, conscious, he had his ears and fingers and he wasn't in Chechnya. He was in Ukraine; in occupied Donetsk but still in Ukraine. And it was such a relief. In some sick way, I felt almost happy that day. I received a message from Viktor Medvedchuk's stepson, Bogdan Marchenko. He sent me a video posted by Medvedchuk's wife, Oksana Marchenko, calling for Aiden and Shaun to be exchanged for her husband. Normally, I would just block him and wouldn't start any conversations with such a person. But the thing is that Shaun was captured a bit later than Aiden and at that moment we had no idea where Shaun was. We were trying to find him but he wasn't in any lists. He wasn't in the list of fallen, wounded or captured marines. So, I asked for proof they had Shaun. First, he sent me some faked evidence. I asked for more, he said he would try to find something but he said I should have no doubt Shaun was captured. And then in an hour or two they let Shaun make a call. After Shaun made a call and we knew he had been captured, I blocked that guy and never spoke to him again.

'I'm pretty sure Bogdan Marchenko was in contact with the FSB. I have no other explanation how Medvedchuk's stepson could possibly know about Aiden's and Shaun's whereabouts. The FSB's goal was to manipulate and psychologically torture us by saying that the guys were going to be executed to make us push for their exchange. Putin was desperate for Medvedchuk.

'There were long unbearable days and weeks of waiting.

But there was nothing new except bullshit propaganda, hate speeches, threats, the kangaroo court, the sham trial and the death penalty. I thought I was ready for this verdict, I didn't expect anything different from those barbarians. But I was wrong. You just can't be ready for things like a death sentence for your lover. Deep inside I knew it was propaganda and they just wanted to exchange our guys for somebody important. But it's easy to be so sure when it's not about the person you love and plan to build your life with. Those were very dark days. Talking to Aiden on the phone made me feel better at some point because I knew he was alive. I kept asking him stupid questions: "Are you fine? Are they treating you properly? Do they feed you and give you enough water? Do they let you take a shower?"

'Of course, he would always say "Everything is fine." I knew he couldn't say anything different but I really wanted to believe he was as well as possible. I can't call it a normal conversation when you know his captors are listening in to every single word he's saying and he's telling only what they want him to tell. It was the same with the propaganda videos. I wanted to see him but it hurt listening to what he was saying. So sometimes I would just switch off the volume. I kept repeating to myself I was very lucky to have the opportunity to hear his voice, to see his videos, even if they were propaganda. I was lucky to know he was alive. Thousands of women didn't have the opportunity to speak to their loved ones or to know they were alive.

'Talking to Larysa, Shaun's wife, helped a lot. We met only once, back in 2020, but had stayed in touch since the very first day of the full-scale war. It's weird how an almost unknown person can become a close friend. We've been through the same hell together and could understand each other with almost no words. There were a couple of times when we got emotional and shared the most terrible fears, but apart from that we were trying to stay strong in front of each other, share every single piece of information we had, support each other, and convince ourselves our boys would come back.

'I was absolutely sure that the Ukrainian Ministry of Defence would never abandon Aiden. I knew that for them he is a Ukrainian defender. The three most terrible moments for me during Aiden's captivity were, first, realizing he had been captured and seeing the pictures and videos of him beaten. Second, the trial and death sentence. And the third terrible moment was seeing him singing the Russian anthem. I couldn't watch it till the end. After seeing him sing that, I had a breakdown for a couple of days.

'But then suddenly it was over. His first words when he called me after he was free were: "Baby, do you know everything I said was bullshit?" And I thought, "Jesus, he went through the hells of Mariupol, captivity, trial, death sentence, and all he can think about is that somebody could believe that bullshit propaganda?"

'That was funny and heartbreaking at the same time. He's got a scar on his forehead just like Harry Potter and I call him "the boy who lived".'

It had been grim for Mum, too.

'The call came in the middle of the night. I was awoken by my phone exploding with noise. Half-asleep I was thinking, "Fuck me, I've set my alarm wrong for work", and drifted back to sleep. Then my phone kept vibrating so I picked it up, the time was two o'clock in the morning. It was Aiden's friends telling me that he had destroyed his phone but he's sent me a message on Facebook. I managed to get through to him and he said he only had a short time to call as there were around two hundred men calling home. My heart was sinking, I could do nothing but re-assure him that I would do anything in my power to keep him alive. Aiden sent me his "proof of life" video. Fuck me, did I cry watching it, my son so brave about to walk into hell. I was not prepared at all for what was coming. His last words to me were: "I love you Mum."

'As soon as I had that video in my hands, I sent it to Brennan and another contact who ran it on his Instagram page. Before I knew it the video had gone viral, all over the world. I sensed Aiden knew what he was doing and this, ultimately, I believe, saved his life.

'Two days later, on our fun day out with my daughter and grandsons, I was shown the propaganda picture on the internet. There in front of me was Aiden's face battered, bruised, his eyes looked like he had been drugged. As a mother I was distressed and nearly passed out. What had those bastards done to him? Anybody who has a child, no matter what age, will fight fire with fire and that was what was about to happen. To see your child tortured, beaten, and paraded on Russian propaganda TV is something that will haunt me for the rest of my life. I'm just a normal mum who works hard.

'I called the Foreign Office and from then on, they were

a big part of our lives. Without their support I would have cracked up. Those dirty Russians, as I will call them, would send me videos of Aiden, his hands bound or in handcuffs, and through Aiden speaking they would tell me to call Boris Johnson, like I had Boris on speed dial. They would try and put pressure on me to give in to their demands. Like fuck I would. His so-called lawyer WhatsApped me at all times of the night, trying to extort £5,000 from me. "You know what," I said, "get stuffed."

'I found myself going into robot mode every day searching on Twitter for Russian news. Every day they were saying, "Aiden would be executed by firing squad", and "I would receive his body parts through the post." Most days, I was distraught, either crying or angry, not knowing what they were doing to my son.

'The one day that makes my blood boil was the day I saw the face of Graham Phillips – I nicknamed him "Fathead Phillips" – with Aiden. I hate the way he portrays himself as a Nottingham man, twenty-six miles away from where we live. How fucking dare he even speak Aiden's name. My message to him was "Fuck you, you creep!"'

It's fair to say that Mum is a fighter. She flagged Phillips' video with YouTube and got it taken down. But, at the time of writing, Phillips is back on Twitter, calling his return a victory for free speech. When he 'interviewed' me, my speech was anything but free – and he knew that. That Twitter should give Graham Phillips a platform continues the psychological agony he caused – causes – me. Here, I ask Elon Musk to kick my torturer off Twitter. Do that now.

The death sentence was a grim day for Mum.

'What else can you do when you have just been told, "We are going to kill your son"? I went on the media, talked to my MP, I fought as hard as I could. But inside, some days I was not thinking rationally. I was driving myself mad, about to have a nervous breakdown. I couldn't eat or sleep. But we as a family pulled together. Strangers sent me letters and flowers, this was overwhelming for me, I was after all just a mum. When Aiden was released, I felt this nightmare was over. Now the truth will come out, what they did to Aiden . . . you reap what you sow and God will make sure of that.'

We Aslins are just an ordinary working-class family from Nottinghamshire. But I like to think that we took on the Kremlin and the Kremlin lost.

Russia's evil war against Ukraine is not over, not by a long chalk. Many of my friends I have written about here in the book are still in captivity, still singing that fucking anthem. I have changed some names to protect their identities. I think about them, often.

I think, too, about my time in a Russian-controlled prison, about the source of all that evil, the man whose picture hung in our cell above the words of that fucking anthem. The war is not over but, I believe, Ukraine will win so long as the West keeps on supporting it properly. And that means Vladimir Putin is in trouble. Big trouble. I am ashamed of much of what I did in captivity, but it is fair to say that I did shout out that Putin is a 'dickhead' – and about that I am rather proud.

Three Four? If I could kill him, I would.

Knifeman? Back in Blighty I went online and found a Ukrainian website with his photo on it. His name is Vladimir Viktorovich Zakharov and, one day, I hope to give evidence against him in The Hague. Likewise, I hope to see Graham Phillips, John Mark Dougan, Popov and Vlad in the dock. Forcing prisoners of war to take part in black propaganda – on pain of torture – is a war crime. I have started legal action against these bad people and this book will form part of the evidence I hope to submit to The Hague when that day comes.

But the figure who troubles me the most is Mr Khorosho – Mr Good. He was, we all thought, a decent man in a bad place. But he was on shift that day when our fellow prisoner was murdered in the next cell along. He could have stopped it. But he did zilch. And that's when evil works.

When good men stand by and do nothing.

And I think about that poor man, hooded, crawling on his hands and knees, being beaten so viciously for so long that the last thing we can hear is the sound of a truncheon clubbing a human body and nothing more.

I don't even know his name.

# Acknowledgements

Much as I don't like Conservative prime ministers, and much as it pains me, I have to thank Boris Johnson and Liz Truss for sticking it to the Kremlin when I was sentenced to death. Thanks, too, to President Volodymyr Zelenskiy for securing my release. I am fully aware that Crown Prince Mohammed bin Salman and Roman Abramovich had their own motives in facilitating my release and that of others: still, it would be churlish not to thank them. My MP, Robert Jenrick, did his bit and I thank him too.

Thanks, too, to Vlad Demchenko for writing the foreword. I have one question for him. So, he arrested John Sweeney on Day Two. Why on earth did he let him go?

I am confident that this book is an honest account of what happened to me. There are times when the precise sequence of events has been hard for me to remember. Please forgive me. But you must understand that taking notes while being tortured in a Russian-controlled prison is not an option.

During the grimmest of times, when the kangaroo court in Donetsk sentenced us all to death, my great good friends

Shaun Pinner and Brahim Saâdoune kept my spirits up. There are no better friends than the ones who look after you when all hope is lost, and I thank them very much.

Every single one of my Ukrainian marine comrades helped me survive the siege of Mariupol and then the hell of captivity. Three stand out: my Kombat or Battalion Commander, Bova, my Ukrainian cellmate Viktor, the lad who taught me the Russian national anthem so I would not get beaten, and my Croatian cellmate, Prebeg, who is the reason I never quite got round to killing myself. To my friends in the Ukrainian marines who are still held by the Russians and their proxies, there is not a day when I do not think of you and I hope one day, soon, you will be freed.

Hostage International supported my mother, Ang, throughout, and thanks to the good people at the Foreign Office, too, who explained what was really happening to my loved ones. Emma Vardy of the BBC went out of her way to keep my family abreast of the latest news before she went on air.

My family were heroes. I must thank my grandmother Pamela, my father Andrew Wood, my sister Shannon and my brother Nathan who stood by me throughout.

My mum Ang fought like a Bengal tiger for my release. Hayley Rogers, her manager, supported her day and night and she was a brick. I am so lucky to have a mother like Ang.

Lastly, and above all, I have to thank Diana. If I am 'the boy who lived', then she is the girl who saved my life.

# About the Authors

**Aiden Aslin** is a British-born resident of Ukraine. Living in Mykolaiv with his fiancée, he joined the Ukrainian Marines in 2018 and was called to the front line ahead of the Russian invasion in February 2022. He was one of over a thousand soldiers who surrendered after the month-long siege at the Mariupol steelworks, whereupon he was singled out for his British passport. His surrender, captivity, treatment and subsequent release received global media attention.

**John Sweeney** is a writer and journalist who, when working for the BBC, challenged dictators, despots, cult leaders, con artists and crooked businessmen for many years. Sweeney has covered wars and chaos in one hundred countries and been undercover to a number of tyrannies, including Chechnya, North Korea and Zimbabwe. The author of fifteen books including the *Sunday Times* bestseller *Killer in the Kremlin*, he reports on the war in Ukraine from his Twitter handle @johnsweeneyroar.